City Government, Salt Lake

Revised ordinances and resolutions of the City Council of Salt Lake

City

in the territory of Utah with congressional and territorial laws on town sites, and

Great Salt Lake City Charter, and amendments

City Government, Salt Lake

Revised ordinances and resolutions of the City Council of Salt Lake City
in the territory of Utah with congressional and territorial laws on town sites, and Great Salt Lake City Charter, and amendments

ISBN/EAN: 9783337301927

Printed in Europe, USA, Canada, Australia, Japan

Cover: Foto ©Suzi / pixelio.de

More available books at **www.hansebooks.com**

REVISED

ORDINANCES

AND

RESOLUTIONS

OF THE

CITY COUNCIL OF SALT LAKE CITY,

IN THE

TERRITORY OF UTAH.

WITH

CONGRESSIONAL AND TERRITORIAL LAWS ON TOWNSITES,

AND

GREAT SALT LAKE CITY CHARTER,

AND AMENDMENTS.

———

PRINTED BY ORDER OF THE CITY COUNCIL.

———

1875.

DESERET NEWS PRINT.

CONTENTS

CHAPTER VII.

CHAPTER VIII.

Relating to Licenses.

CHAPTER IX.

v

CHAPTER X.

CHAPTER XXI.

CHAPTER XXII.

CHAPTER XXIII.

CHAPTER XXIV.

CHAPTER XXV.

CHAPTER XXVI.

CHAPTER XXVII.

CHAPTER XXVIII.

CHAPTER XXIX.

CHAPTER XXX.

CHAPTER XXXI.

CHAPTER XXXII.

CHAPTER XXXIII.

CHAPTER XXXIV.

CHAPTER XXXV.

CHAPTER XXXVI.

CHAPTER XXXVII.

CHAPTER XXXVIII.

CHAPTER XXXIX.

CHAPTER XL.

2

CHAPTER L.

CHAPTER LI.

INDEX

TO CONGRESSIONAL AND TERRITORIAL ACTS ON TOWN-
SITES.

INDEX

TO GREAT SALT LAKE CITY CHARTER AND AMEND-
MENTS.

———◆———

XIV

INDEX

TO REVISED ORDINANCES AND RESOLUTIONS.

3.

XXIV

AN ACT

FOR THE RELIEF OF THE INHABITANTS OF CITIES AND TOWNS
UPON THE PUBLIC LANDS.

---

*Be it enacted by the Senate and House of Representatives of
the United States of America in Congress assembled,*

That whenever any portion of the public lands of the
United States have been or shall be settled upon and occupied as
a town site, and therefore not subject to entry under the agricul-
tural pre-emption laws, it shall be lawful, in case such town
shall be incorporated, for the corporate authorities thereof, and if not incorporated, for the judge of the county court
for the county in which such town may be situated, to
enter at the proper land office, and at the minimum price, the
land so settled and occupied, in trust for the several use and
benefit of the occupants thereof, according to their respective interests; the execution of which trust, as to the disposal of the
lots in such town, and the proceeds of the sales thereof, to be
conducted under such rules and regulations as may be prescribed
by the legislative authority of the State or Territory in which
the same may be situated.

Provided: That the entry of the land intended by this act to
be made shall be made, or a declaratory statement of the purpose
of the inhabitants to enter it as a town site under this act shall be
filed with the register of the proper land office, prior to the com-
mencement of the public sale of the body of land in which it is
included, and that the entry or declaratory statement shall include only such land as is actually occupied by the town and the
title to which is in the United States. If upon surveyed lands
the entry shall in its exterior limit be made in conformity to the
legal subdivisions of the public lands authorized by the act of
twenty-fourth April, one thousand eight hundred and twenty;
and where the inhabitants are in number one hundred and less

[margin notes: Town authorities, etc., may enter public lands occupied as town sites. Trust, how executed. Entry, etc., when to be made. To include what. Upon surveyed lands.]

than two hundred, shall embrace not exceeding three hundred and twenty acres; and in cases where the inhabitants of such town are more than two hundred and less than one thousand, shall embrace not exceeding six hundred and forty acres; and where the number of inhabitants is one thousand and over one thousand, shall embrace not exceeding twelve hundred and eighty acres.

Amount of land that may be entered.

Proviso.

Provided: That for each additional one thousand inhabitants, not exceeding five thousand in all, a further grant of three hundred and twenty acres shall be allowed. *And provided further,* That in any Territory in which a land office may not have been established, declaratory statements as hereinbefore provided may be filed with the surveyor-general of the surveying district in which the lands are situate, who shall transmit said declaratory statement to the general land office. *And provided, further,* That any act of said trustees not made in conformity to the rules and regulations herein alluded to shall be void; effect to be given to the foregoing provisions according to such regulations as may be prescribed by the Secretary of the Interior. *And provided further,* That the provisions of this act shall not apply to military or other reservations heretofore made by the United States, nor to reservations for lighthouses, custom houses, mints, or such other public purposes as the interests of the United States may require, whether held under reservations through the land office by title derived from the crown of Spain, or otherwise. *And provided further,* That no title shall be acquired, under the provisions of this act, to any mine of gold, silver, cinnabar, or copper.

Approved March 2, 1867.

Where there is no land office, statements to be filed where.

Certain acts of trustees to be void.

Regulations.

This act not to apply to certain reservations.

Nor to mines of gold &c.

AN ACT

TO AMEND AN ACT ENTITLED "AN ACT FOR THE RELIEF OF THE INHABITANTS OF CITIES AND TOWNS UPON THE PUBLIC LANDS," APPROVED MARCH TWO, EIGHTEEN HUNDRED AND SIXTY-SEVEN.

Be it enacted by the Senate and House of Representatives of the United States of America in Congress assembled:

That the inhabitants of any town located on the public land of the United States may avail themselves, if the town authorities elect so to do, of the provisions of the act of March two, eighteen hundred and sixty-seven, entitled "An Act for the relief of the inhabitants of cities and towns upon the public lands." *Provided,* This act shall not prevent the issuance of patents to persons who have made, or may make, entries and elect to proceed under existing laws. *And provided further,* That no title under said act of March two, eighteen hundred and sixty-seven, shall be acquired to any valid mining claim or possession held under the existing laws of Congress. *Provided also,* That in addition to the minimum price of the lands included in any town-site entered under the provisions of this act, and "An Act for the relief of the inhabitants of cities and towns upon the public lands," approved March two, eighteen hundred and sixty-seven, there shall be paid by the parties availing themselves of the provisions of said acts all costs of surveying and platting any such town site, and expenses incident thereto incurred by the United States, before any patent shall issue therefor.

Approved June 8, 1868.

[Sidenotes: Inhabitants of towns, etc., may enter public lands. Patents to issue to those making entries under existing laws. No title given to any valid mining claim. Cost of survey, etc., to be paid.]

A N   A C T

FOR THE RELIEF OF THE INHABITANTS OF SALT LAKE CITY,
IN THE TERRITORY OF UTAH.

Be it enacted by the Senate and House of Representatives of the United States of America in Congress assembled:

Authorities of Salt Lake City may enter public lands, and to what amount under act of 1867.

That the words "not exceeding five thousand in all" contained in an Act intitled " An Act for the relief of the inhabitants of cities and towns upon the public lands," approved March two, eighteen hundred and sixty-seven, shall not apply to Salt Lake City, in the Territory of Utah ; but said act shall be so amended and construed in its application to said city that lands may be entered as provided in said act for the full number of inhabitants contained in said city not exceeding fifteen thousand ;

School section may be included.

and as the city covers school section number thirty-six, in township number one north, of range number one west, the same may be embraced in such entry, and indemnity shall be given

Indemnity therefor.

therefor when a grant shall be made by Congress of sections sixteen and thirty-six, in the Territory of Utah, for school purposes.

Approved July 1, 1870.

AN ACT

PRESCRIBING RULES AND REGULATIONS FOR THE EXECUTION
OF THE TRUST ARISING UNDER AN ACT OF CONGRESS, EN-
TITLED "AN ACT FOR THE RELIEF OF THE INHABITANTS
OF CITIES AND TOWNS UPON THE PUBLIC LANDS," AP-
PROVED MARCH 2, 1867.

SEC. 1. Be it enacted by the Governor and Legislative Assembly of the Territory of Utah: That when the corporate authorities of any town or city, or the Probate Judge of any county
in this Territory, (who, for the purposes of this Act, and of receiving and executing the trust declared by the Act of Congress Entered at
hereinafter mentioned, shall be deemed and is hereby designated land office
as the Judge of the county court for such county), in which any
town or city may be situated, shall have entered at the proper
land office the land or any part of the land settled and occupied
as the site of such town, pursuant to and by virtue of the provisions of the Act of Congress entitled "An Act for the relief of
the inhabitants of cities and towns upon the public lands," approved March 2, 1867, and any amendments that may be made
thereto, it shall be the duty of such corporate authorities or
judge (as the case may be), and they are hereby directed and re- Convey
quired, to dispose of and convey the title to such land, or to the title.
several blocks, lots, parcels or shares thereof to the persons en- Deeds exe-
titled thereto, to be ascertained as hereinafter prescribed. Deeds cuted by
of conveyance for the same shall be executed by the Mayor of and Judge
the city or town, under the seal of the corporation, when the of Pro-
entry shall be made by the corporate authorities of such city or bate.
town; and by the Judge of Probate when the entry shall be
made by such Judge, and in all cases said deeds shall be ac-
knowledged before and certified by an officer competent under
the laws of this Territory to take acknowledgments of deeds of
conveyance of real estate.

SEC. 2. That within thirty days after the entry of any such

Notice of entry. lands, the corporate authorities, or judge, entering the same, shall give public notice of such entry in at least five public places within such town or city, and by publishing such notice in some newspaper printed and published in this Territory, having a general circulation in such town or city. Said notice shall be published once in each week for at least three successive months, and shall contain an accurate description of the lands so entered as stated in the certificate of entry or duplicate receipt received from the officers of the land office.

SEC. 3. That each and every person or association, or company of persons, or persons or corporation claiming to be the

Each claimant to sign a statement for filing. rightful owner of possession, occupant or occupants, or to be entitled to the occupancy or possession of such lands, or to any lot, block, share or parcel thereof, shall, within six months after the first publication of such notice, in person, or by his, her or their agent or attorney, sign a statement in writing, containing an accurate description of the particular parcel or parts of land in which he, she or they claim to have an interest, and the specific right, interest or estate therein, which he, she or they claim to be entitled to receive, and deliver the same to the clerk of the Probate Court of the county in which such town or city is situated, and the clerk of said court shall enter such statement in a book to be kept for that purpose, and file and preserve the same in his office, noting the day of filing. The filing of which statement shall be considered as notice, to all persons claiming any interest in the lands described therein, of the claim of the

Extending time of filing. party filing the same, and all persons failing to make and deliver such statement within the time limited in this section shall be forever barred the right of claiming or recovering such land, or any interest or estate therein, or in any part, parcel or share thereof in any court of law or equity. *Provided,* That when good cause is shown why such statement could not be filed within the time herein specified, the Judge may extend the time not exceeding one year from the first publication of said notice.

SEC. 4. That if at the expiration of six months after the first publication of the notice as aforesaid, it shall be found by

Adverse claimants. the statements filed that there are adverse claimants to any tract or parcel of land it shall be the duty of the Judge of Probate to cause notice to be served upon said claimants or their agent or attorney, (taking up each case in the order of filing) to appear before the Probate Court of the county in which such tract or parcel of land may be situated, and prosecute their claim upon a day to be appointed by said court, not less than five nor more than thirty days from the service of such notice; the statements filed as aforesaid shall stand in said court in the place of pleadings, and an issue be made thereon ; and on the day set for the hearing, the judge shall proceed to hear the proof adduced and allegations of the parties, and decide according to the justice of the case. The court shall cause full minutes of the testimony to be kept, which shall be preserved with the papers in the case, and be entered upon the records of said court the decision at length. If either party shall feel aggrieved at the decision of said court, he, she or they shall have the right of appeal to the District Court as in other cases, and upon the perfection of such appeal the court shall cause the testimony and written proofs adduced, together with the statements of the parties and the judgment of the court to be certified by the District Court, to be there tried anew without pleadings except as above provided.

(margin: Appear before the Probate Court.)

(margin: Appeal to District Court.)

SEC. 5. That after the expiration of the six months, provided in section three of this act, for filing statements in cases where there are no adverse claimants, the court shall cause summons to be issued and served upon the party filing such statement, or his, her or their agent, requiring him, her or them, or their agent or attorney, to appear before said court upon a day designated, not less than three nor more than ten days from service of such summons, and to make proofs in support of such statement, full minutes of which shall be kept; and the court, if satisfied from the proofs of the validity of such claim, shall cause judgment to be entered of record, and the minutes of the proofs to be preserved as required in section four of this act; and thereupon shall certify the fact to the Mayor of the city or town, (in cases where the corporate authorities shall have made the entry), who shall make the party claimant a deed of conveyance for the tract or parcel of land so adjudged to him, her or them. If the court shall decide against the validity of such claim, the decision shall in like manner be entered on record and the minutes of testimony preserved, and in all cases appeals and writs of error shall be allowed from the decision of such court to any party in interest, as in other cases. In cases where the entry shall have been made by the Probate Judge, the conveyance shall be made

(margin: Court to certify to Mayor, who shall make deed.)

(margin: Decision against validity.)

by him in accordance with the judgment entered as aforesaid; each case shall be taken up by the court in the order in which the statements have been filed. If the Judge of Probate shall

Probate Judge to file in adjoining county. be a claimant of lands in any city or town in his county he may file the statement required in section three of this act in the Probate Court of an adjoining county, who shall cause notice thereof to be given to all adverse claimants, if any, and to the Mayor of such city or town, and in cases of unincorporated towns, to the Justice of Peace of the precinct in which such town may be situated; and the Probate Court of such adjoining county shall proceed in the examination and decision of the case as provided in this act as in other cases, and upon the certificate of said court a deed to the lands shall be made to the party or parties entitled thereto, as provided in this section; *Provided,* That if there shall be an adverse claimant or claimants to any tract so claimed by any Judge of Probate, and a statement shall have

Final judgment to authorize Mayor to make conveyance. been filed as required in section three of this act, the Probate Court shall cause the same to be certified to the Probate Court of the county selected to hear and determine such case. A copy of the final judgment in all cases appealed under this act shall authorize the Mayor or Judge to make conveyance as hereinbefore provided in other cases, or withhold it according to such judgment. In cases where the Judge of Probate, who shall hold the lands in trust, is a party claimant to any portion thereof, and the final judgment of the proper tribunal shall be in his favor, such decision shall operate to discharge the trust in the portion of land so assigned to him. If the Mayor of any city or town shall be a claimant of any lands in such city or town, the Recorder of

The Recorder to execute deed to Mayor. such city shall, upon the certificate of the Probate Court, made as in case of other claimants, execute a deed of conveyance to such Mayor for the lands finally adjudged to him by the court under the same rules and regulations as prescribed in other cases.

SEC. 6. That a change of venue, as in suits at law, shall be allowed in all cases arising under this act.

SEC. 7. That within thirty days after the expiration of the six months prescribed in section three for filing statements, the corporate authorities or Judge holding the title to the lands described in the notice published, as required in section two, shall make a statement in writing, containing a true account of all moneys by them or him expended in the acquisition of the title and the administration or execution of the trust to that time, in-

cluding the money paid by them or him for the purchase of said
lands, all necessary traveling expenses, all moneys paid for publishing and posting notices, and for all other necessary and proper expenses incident to such trust to that time, which statement shall be filed in the office of the clerk of the Probate Court
of the county in which such town or city may be situated, and
shall be open for inspection by all persons interested during ordinary business hours.

Statement
of expens-
es to be
filed with
clerk of
Probate
Court
open for
inspec-
tion.

SEC. 8. That before the corporate authorities or Judge holding
any such lands in trust, as aforesaid, shall be required to execute,
acknowledge, or deliver any deed of conveyance thereof, as hereinbefore provided, to any person or persons claiming and adjudged to be entitled to such deed, such person or persons shall
pay, or tender to the Mayor or Judge, as the case may be, the
sum of money chargeable on the part thereof to be conveyed by
such deed, to be ascertained by taking the whole amount of the cost
of the land of which it is a part, and expenses stated in the account,
as prescribed in section seven, in the proportion which the area of
such lot shall bear to the whole amount of land entered, after
deducting the area of all streets, alleys, and public grounds in
such city or town, and the reasonable charges for preparing, executing, and acknowledging such deed, including the interest on
the money expended: *Provided*, errors in measurement or com-
putation shall not invalidate any proceeding under this act.

Payment
of lands
to be
made be-
fore receiv-
ing deed
therefor.

SEC. 9. That whenever the title to such lands shall be held
by the corporate authorities of any town or city, all lands designated for public use by such corporate authorities, as streets,
lanes, avenues, alleys, parks, commons and public grounds,
shall vest in and be held by the corporation absolutely, and shall
not be claimed adversely by any person or persons whomsoever.
And the Judge of Probate who shall have entered any lands in
trust for any town or city which may afterwards become incorporated, shall, under the same conditions, convey by deed to the
corporation thereof the lands designated for the use of the public
as aforesaid. That in case of the death or disability of the Judge
of Probate, or Mayor, who may have entered the lands in trust for
any town or city under the law of Congress as aforesaid before
the complete execution of such trust, the same trust shall vest
in his successor in office, who shall proceed with the execution
of the same in the same manner and under the same conditions
imposed by this Act upon the Judge or Mayor receiving the
trust in the first instance.

Judge of
Probate to
convey
deed for
lands for
public
use.

SEC. 10. If there shall remain any unclaimed lands within
the limits of such city or town after the expiration of six months
from the publication of the notice provided in section three, the
corporate authorities, in cases where the lands shall have been entered by them, and the Judge of Probate in cases where the lands
shall have been entered by him, shall cause the same to be surveyed and laid out into suitable blocks and lots, and shall reserve
such portions as may be deemed necessary for public squares,
school-houses or hospital lots, and shall cause all necessary
streets, roads, lanes and alleys to be laid out through the same, a
plat of which, properly certified, shall be recorded in the Recorder's office of the county in which the same may be situated;
and the Mayor of such city or town, or Judge as aforesaid may
sell the lots and blocks so laid out—and not reserved for public
use—in suitable parcels, to possessors of adjoining lands or to
other citizens of such city or town, at a price not less than five
dollars per acre, or fraction of an acre; and in case two or more
persons apply for the same tract, they shall sell the same by auction to the highest bidder. And if any such lands remain unsold at the end of three months from the date of filing the plat
thereof for record, as required herein, the corporate authorities
or Judge as aforesaid, shall have power and authority to sell
such vacant lands at public and private sale in such manner
and on such terms as they may deem advisable for the best interests of the city or town, and shall give deeds therefor to the
several purchasers.

*Unclaim-
ed lands
reserved
for public
squares,
etc.*

*To be sold
at public
or private
sale.*

SEC. 11. That all moneys arising from the sale of lands
entered in trust by the corporate authorities of any city or town,
or by the Judge of Probate under the said Act of Congress, after
deducting all moneys paid for said lands and the expenses incurred in the management and execution of the trust, shall be paid
into the County Treasury, for the support and maintenance of
common schools in said city or town, to be applied and expended
in such manner as shall be provided by law.

*Money to
be paid in-
to County
Treasury.*

SEC. 12. That the several officers hereinafter mentioned
may charge and collect the following fees for their service under
this Act, viz: The Judge of Probate for hearing the proofs and
giving judgment in each contested case, one dollar and fifty
cents; in each case where there is no contest, one dollar; for
preparing and executing each deed, fifty cents, exclusive of revenue stamps; for each certificate embodying a copy of the record

*Rate of
fees to be
charged.*

of the decision of the court, twenty-five cents. The Clerk of the Probate Court for each summons or subpœna, twenty-five cents; for filing each statement and entering the same, ten cents; swearing each witness, five cents; for certificate and seal to each certificate of title, twenty-five cents; for each certificate of acknowledgment of deed, with seal, twenty-five cents; the Mayor of the City, for preparing and executing each deed of conveyance, fifty cents, exclusive of revenue stamps; the Sheriff or Constable for serving process of summons or subpœna, twenty-five cents; for each mile actually traveled in serving process, ten cents.

Approved, Feb. 17, 1869

GREAT SALT LAKE CITY

CHARTER

AND AMENDMENTS.

An ACT Incorporating Great Salt Lake City.

SEC. 1.—Be it enacted by the Governor and Legislative As- Bounda-
sembly of the Territory of Utah: That all that district of country ries.
embraced in the following boundaries, to wit:—Beginning at a
point one hundred and thirty-six rods north of the Hot Spring,
thence west to the west bank of the Jordan river, thence up the
west bank thereof to a point directly west from the south-west
corner of the five acre lots according to the present survey, thence
east along the south line of said lots to the southeast corner
thereof, thence east nine hundred rods, thence north to a point
directly east of the beginning, thence west to the aforesaid place
of beginning, shall be known and designated by the name and
style of Great Salt Lake City; and the inhabitants thereof are
hereby constituted a body corporate and politic, by the name and Name.
style aforesaid, with perpetual succession; and shall have and use
a common seal, which they may change and alter at their pleasure.

SEC. 2.—The inhabitants of said City, by the name and style Powers.
aforesaid, shall have power to sue and be sued, to plead and be
impleaded, defend and be defended in all Courts of law and equity
and in all actions whatsoever; to purchase, receive, hold, sell

A

lease, convey and dispose of property real and personal for the benefit of said City, both within and without its corporate boundaries; to improve and protect such property, and do all other things in relation thereto as natural persons.

Wards.
SEC. 3.—Said City shall be divided into five Municipal Wards, whose boundaries shall be as prescribed by the City ordinance.

Government
SEC. 4.—The Municipal Government of said City is hereby vested in a City Council, to be composed of a Mayor, five Aldermen, one from each Ward, and nine Councilors, who shall have the qualifications of electors in said City, and shall be chosen by the qualified voters thereof, and shall hold their offices for two years, and until their successors are elected and qualified.

Elections.
SEC. 5.—An election shall be held on the second Monday of February next, and every two years thereafter on said day, at which there shall be elected one Mayor, five Aldermen, nine

Officers.
Councillors, one Marshal, one Treasurer and one Recorder; and the persons respectively receiving the highest number of votes cast in the city for said offices shall be declared elected. When two or more candidates for an elective office shall have an equal number of votes for the same office, the election shall be determined by the City Council.

First Election.
SEC. 6.—The first election under this act shall be conducted in the following manner, to wit:—The County Clerk of Great Salt Lake County shall cause notice of the time and place, and the number and kind of officers to be chosen, to be advertised in some newspaper of said city, or posted up in five public places therein, at least ten days previous to said election. Three Judges shall be selected by the Probate Judge of Great Salt Lake County, at least one week previous to the day of election; said Judges shall choose two Clerks; and the Judges and Clerks, before entering upon their duties, shall take and subscribe an oath or affirmation for the faithful discharge thereof. At the first election so held, the polls shall be opened at eight o'clock a. m., and shall close at six o'clock p. m. At the close of the election the Judges shall seal up the ballot box and the list of the names of the electors, and transmit the same, within two days, to the County Clerk of Great Salt Lake County. As soon as the returns are received, the County Clerk, in the presence of the Probate Judge, shall unseal and examine them, and furnish, within five days, to each person having the highest number of votes, a certificate of his election.

Subsequent Elections.
SEC. 7.—The manner of conducting and voting at all subsequent elections to be held under this act, and contesting the same,

the keeping of the poll lists, canvassing the votes, and certifying the returns, and all other things relating thereto, shall be as provided by city ordinance.

SEC. 8.—There shall be appointed an Assessor and Collector, an Auditor of Public Accounts, a Supervisor of Streets, a Surveyor, an Attorney, a Board of School Inspectors, a Sealer of Weights and Measures, a Sexton or keeper of burial grounds, a Chief of Police, Inspectors, Measurers and Weighers, and such other officers and agents as the City Council may from time to time direct and appoint. *Officers Appointed.*

SEC. 9.—Every person elected or appointed to any office under the provisions of this act may be removed from such office by a vote of two-thirds of the City Council; and no officer shall be removed except for cause, nor unless furnished with the charges; and shall have an opportunity of being heard in his defence; and the Council shall have power to compel the attendance of witnesses and the production of papers when necessary for the purpose of such trial, and shall proceed, within ten days, to hear and determine upon the merits of the case; and if such officer shall neglect to appear and answer to such charges, then the Council may declare the office vacant. All officers appointed by the Council may be removed at any time by vote, at discretion of two-thirds, of said Council; and any officer may be suspended until the disposition of charges preferred against him. *Removals.*

SEC. 10.—Whenever any vacancy shall happen by the death, resignation, or removal of any officer, such vacancy may be filled by the City Council; and every person elected or appointed to an elective, judicial or administrative office, shall, before he enters upon the duties thereof, take and subscribe an oath or affirmation that he will support the Constitution of the United States, the laws of this Territory and the Ordinances of this city, and that he will well and truly perform all the duties of his office to the best of his knowledge and ability; and shall file the same, duly certified by the officer before whom it was taken, with the City Recorder. *Vacancies, how filled.* *Oath.*

SEC. 11.—Any person or persons illegally voting at any election under this act, shall be punishable according to law regulating general elections. *Illegal voting.*

SEC. 12.—The Mayor shall, before he enters upon the duties of his office, in addition to the usual oath, swear or affirm that he will devote so much of his time to the duties of his office as an efficient and faithful discharge thereof may require; and shall from *Oath of Mayor.*

time to time give the Council such information and recommend such measures as he may deem advantageous to the city.

Qualification and duties of Mayor and Aldermen. SEC. 13.—The Mayor and Aldermen shall be conservators of the peace within the limits of the city, and shall give bonds and qualify as other Justices of the Peace; and, when so qualified, shall possess the same power and jurisdiction, both in civil and criminal cases arising under the laws of the Territory, and may be commissioned as justices of the Peace in and for said city by the Governor. They shall account for and pay over to the city Treasurer, within three months, all fines and forfeitures received by them in their judicial capacity; and they shall each keep a docket, subject at all times to the inspection of the City Council and all other parties interested.

Jurisdiction. SEC. 14.—The Mayor and Aldermen shall have exclusive jurisdiction in all cases arising under the ordinances of the city, and issue such process as may be necessary to carry such ordinances into execution and effect.

Recorder. SEC. 15.—It shall be the duty of the Recorder to make and keep accurate records of all ordinances made by the City Council and all their proceedings in a corporate capacity; which record shall at all times be open to the inspection of the electors of the Duties. city and all other parties interested. He shall have and keep a plat of all surveys within the city, and record all deeds, transfers or other instruments of writing that may be presented to him for that purpose; and he is hereby authorized to take the acknowledgment of deeds, transfers and other instruments of writing, and shall perform such other duties as may be required of him by city ordinance.

Marshal. SEC. 16.—The Marshal shall perform such duties as shall be prescribed by the City Council for the preservation of the public peace. All process issued by the Mayor or an Alderman shall be Duties. directed to the Marshal or his deputy; and in the execution thereof he shall be governed by such rules and regulations as may be provided by city ordinance, and shall be the principal ministerial officer.

Treasurer. SEC. 17.—The Treasurer shall receive all moneys belonging to the city, and shall keep an accurate account of all receipts and expenditures in such manner as the City Council shall direct. Duties. He shall pay all moneys that may come to his hand, by virtue of his office, upon orders signed by the Auditor of Public Accounts, and shall report to the City Council a true account of his receipts and disbursements, as they may require.

SEC. 18.—The City Council, a majority of whom shall form a quorum to transact business, shall meet at such times and places as they may direct; and the Mayor, when present, shall preside at said meetings and have a casting vote. In the absence of the Mayor, any Alderman present may be appointed to preside, in such manner as shall be provided by the City Council. *City Council.*

SEC. 19.—The City Council shall hold stated meetings, and the Mayor or any two Aldermen may call special meetings, by notice to each of the members of said Council, served personally or left at their usual place of abode. Said Council shall determine the rules of its own proceedings, and be judge of the election and qualification of its own members. *Meetings*

SEC. 20.—The City Council shall have the management and control of the finances and property, real, personal and mixed, belonging to the corporation. *Powers*

SEC. 21.—The City Council is hereby empowered within the jurisdiction of the city, by ordinance and enforcement thereof, to prevent, punish or prohibit every kind of fraudulent device and practice; all descriptions of gaming, playing at dice, cards or other games of chance, with or without betting. *Further powers.*

SEC. 22.—To license, tax, regulate, suppress or prohibit billiard tables, pin alleys, nine or ten pin alleys, or tables and ball alleys; to suppress or restrain bawdy and other disorderly houses and groceries; to authorize the destruction and demolition of all instruments and devices used for the purpose of gaming; to prevent any riot, noise, disturbance or disorderly assemblage; and to restrain and punish vagrants, mendicants, street beggars and prostitutes. *May license, tax and regulate.*

SEC. 23.—To regulate the selling or giving away of any ardent spirits or other intoxicating liquors by any storekeeper, grocer or trader, to be drunk in any shop, store, grocery, outhouse, yard, garden or other place within the city, except by persons or at places duly licensed; to forbid the selling or giving away of ardent spirits or other intoxicating liquors to any child, apprentice or servant, without the consent of his or her parent, guardian, master or mistress, or to any Indian. *Regulate liquor traffic*

SEC. 24.—To license, regulate or restrain the manufacturers, sellers or venders of spirituous and fermented liquors, tavern-keepers, dram or tippling shop keepers, grocers and keepers of ordinaries, boarding, victualling or coffee houses, restaurants, *Hotels and Saloons*

saloons or other houses or places for the selling or giving away of wines or other liquors, whether ardent, vinous or fermented.

Exhibitions. SEC. 25.—To regulate, license, suppress or prohibit all exhibitions of common showmen, shows of every kind, concerts or other musical entertainments, exhibitions of natural or artificial curiosities, caravans, circuses, theatrical performances and all other exhibitions and amusements.

Amusements. SEC. 26.—To prevent or regulate the rolling of hoops, playing at ball, flying of kites or any other amusement or practice having a tendency to annoy persons passing in the streets or on the sidewalks, or to frighten teams or horses.

Fast Riding. SEC. 27.—To prevent horse-racing, immoderate riding or driving in the streets, and to authorize their being stopped by any person; to punish or prohibit the abuse of animals; to compel persons to put up posts in front of their lots to fasten their horses or other animals; to compel the fastening of horses, mules, oxen or other animals attached to vehicles, while standing or remaining in the street.

Hitching Posts.

Encumbering streets. SEC. 28.—To prevent the encumbering of the streets or sidewalks, lanes, alleys, and public grounds with carriages, tents, wagons, carts, sleighs, horses or other animals, sleds, wheelbarrows, boxes, lumber, timber, firewood, posts, awnings, signs, adobies or any material or substance whatever.

Cattle at large. SEC. 29.—To restrain, regulate or prohibit the running at large of cattle, horses, mules, sheep, swine, goats and all kinds of poultry; and to authorize the distraining, impounding or sale of the same, for the penalty and costs incurred thereby; and to impose penalties for any violation of city ordinance in relation thereto; and to tax, prevent or regulate the keeping of dogs, and to authorize the destruction of the same, when at large, contrary to city ordinance.

Health regulations. SEC. 30.—To compel the owner or occupant of any grocery, cellar, tallow-chandler shop, soap-factory, tannery, stable, barn, privy, sewer, or any unwholesome place, to cleanse, remove or abate the same from time to time, as often as may be necessary for the health, comfort and convenience of the inhabitants of said city.

Health regulations. SEC. 31.—To direct the location and management of and regulate breweries and tanneries; and to direct the location management and construction of, and restrain or prohibit within the city, distilleries, slaughtering establishments and establishments for steaming and rendering lard, oil, tallow, offal and such

other substances as can or may be rendered; and all establishments or places where nauseous, offensive or unwholesome business may be carried on.

SEC. 32.—To direct or prohibit the location and management Dangerous
of houses for the storing of gunpowder, tar, pitch, rosin or other articles.
combustible and dangerous materials within the city, and to
regulate the keeping and conveying of gunpowder, and the use
of candles and lights in barns, stables or outhouses.

SEC. 33.—To compel persons to keep the snow and ice from Clearing
the sidewalks in front of the premises owned or occupied by sidewalks.
them on East Temple Street, from the Temple Block South to
the intersection with Second South Street.

SEC. 34.—To abate or remove nuisances, and punish the Nuisances
authors thereof, by penalties of fine and imprisonment; and to
define and declare what are nuisances, and authorize and direct
the summary abatement thereof; and to abate all nuisances
which are or may be injurious to the public health, peace or
good order.

SEC. 35.—To prevent any person from bringing, depositing or Offal.
having within the limits of the city any dead carcass or any
other unwholesome substance, and to require the removal or
destruction of the same by any person who shall have placed or
caused to be placed upon or near his premises or near any of the
streams of this city any such substances, or any putrid or unsound beef, pork, or fish, hides or skins of any kind; and, on his
default, to authorize the removal or destruction by any officer of
said city.

SEC. 36.—To exclusively control, regulate, repair, amend and Streets.
clear the streets, alleys, bridges, side-walks or cross-walks; and
open, widen, straighten or vacate streets and alleys, and put
drains or ditches and sewers therein; and prevent the encumbering of the streets in any manner, and protect the same from any
encroachment and injury.

SEC. 37.—To lay out, improve and regulate the public Public
grounds belonging to the city; to direct and regulate the plant- Grounds.
ing and preserving trees in the streets and public grounds; and
to regulate the fencing of lots within the bounds of the city.

SEC. 38.—To prevent the ringing of bells, blowing of horns Street
and bugles, crying of goods and all other noises, performances noises.
and devices tending to the collection of persons on the streets or
side-walks by auctioneers and others, for the purpose of business,
amusement or otherwise.

Bathing.   SEC. 39.—To regulate and determine the times and places of bathing and swimming in the river or other waters in and adjoining said city, and to prevent any obscene or indecent exhibition, exposure or conduct.

Quarantine.   SEC. 40.—To make regulations to prevent the introduction of contagious diseases into the city; to make quarantine laws and enforce the same within the city and around it, not exceeding twelve miles next beyond the bounds thereof.

Licenses.   SEC. 41.—To grant and issue licenses, and direct the manner of issuing and registering thereof, and the fees to be paid therefor. Bonds may be taken, on the granting of licenses, for the due observance of the ordinances or regulations of the City Council.

Mercantile Licenses.   SEC. 42.—To license, tax and regulate merchants and retailers, auctioneers, distillers, brewers, brokers, pawnbrokers and money changers, and to impose duties upon the sale of goods at auction.

Pedlers.   SEC. 43.—To license, tax, regulate or suppress hawkers and pedlers.

Butchers.   SEC. 44.—To regulate and license or prohibit butchers, and to revoke their licenses for malconduct in the course of trade, and to regulate, license and restrain the sale of fresh meat and vegetables in the city; and restrain and punish the forestalling of poultry, fruit and eggs.

Markets.   SEC. 45.—To establish and regulate markets and other public buildings, and provide for their erection, determine their location, and authorize their erection in the streets, avenues or any other public place or places in the city, and not exceeding four miles beyond the bounds thereof.

Census Statistics.   SEC. 46.—To provide for taking the enumeration of the inhabitants of the city; to regulate the burial of the dead, and registration of births and deaths, to direct the returning and keeping of bills of mortality; and to impose penalties on physicians, sextons and others for any default in the premises.

Watchmen.   SEC. 47.—To appoint watchmen and policemen, and prescribe their duties and powers.

Lumber.   SEC. 48.—To regulate the measuring and inspection of lumber, shingles, timber, posts, staves and heading, and all building materials and all kinds of mechanical work; and appoint one or more inspectors therefor.

Hay.   SEC. 49.—To regulate the weighing and place and manner of selling hay.

SEC. 50.—To regulate the inspection of tobacco, also of flour, Provisions meal, pork, beef and other provisions, and salt to be sold in barrels, hogsheads and other packages.

SEC. 51.—To regulate the measuring of wood and weighing Wood. of coal, and the place and manner of selling the same.

SEC. 52.—To regulate the inspection of whisky and other Liquors. liquors to be sold in barrels, hogsheads or other vessels.

SEC. 53.—To appoint inspectors, weighers and guagers, and Inspectors regulate their duties and prescribe their fees.

SEC. 54.—To require every merchant, retailer, trader and Weights dealer in merchandise or property of any description, which is and Measold by measure or weight, to cause their weights and measures sures. to be sealed by the City Sealer and to be subject to his inspection; the standard of which weights and measures shall be conformable to those established by law.

SEC. 55.—To establish, make and regulate public pumps, Water wells, cisterns, hydrants and reservoirs; to distribute, control and Works. so regulate the waters flowing into the city throughout such channels as may be most advantageous, and to prevent the unnecessary waste of water.

SEC. 56.— To erect street lamps and regulate the lighting Street' thereof; and from time to time create, alter and extend lamp Lamps districts.

SEC. 57.—To establish and regulate public pounds. Pounds.

SEC. 58.—To regulate and license ferries. Ferries.

SEC. 59.—To authorize the taking up and providing for the Education safe keeping and education, for such periods of time as may be expedient, of all children who are destitute of all proper parental care, wandering about the streets, committing mischief and growing up in mendicancy, ignorance, idleness and vice.

SEC. 60.—To borrow money on the credit of the city: Provi- Borrow ded, that the interest on the aggregate of all the sums borrowed money. and outstanding, shall not exceed one-fourth of the city revenue arising from taxes assessed within the corporation during the preceding year.

SEC. 61.—The City Council shall have power to make, publish, Ordiordain, amend and repeal all such ordinances, by-laws, or police nances. regulations, not contrary to the Constitution of the United States and the laws of this Territory, for the good government and order of the city, as may be necessary and expedient to carry into effect the powers vested in the City Council or any officer of said city by this act; and enforce observance of all rules, ordnances, reso-

Prescribe penalties.

lutions, by-laws and police and other regulations, made in pursuance of this act, by penalties not exceeding one hundred dollars for any offence against the same, or imprisonment not exceeding six months or both.

Taxes.

SEC. 62.—The City Council shall have power within the city, by ordinance, to annually levy and collect taxes on the assessed value of all real and personal estate or property in the city; made taxable by the laws of the Territory, for the following named purposes, to wit:—Not to exceed five mills on the dollar to defray the contingent expenses of the city. Not to exceed five mills on the dollar to open, improve and keep in repair the streets of the city. Not to exceed one and a quarter mills on the dollar to control the waters of said city; and they shall annually apportion and apply said taxes as shall in their judgment be deemed most expedient.

Taxes.

SEC. 63.—When the City Council shall deem it expedient for any especial purpose to borrow money, the interest on which shall not exceed one fourth of the city revenue arising from taxes of the preceding year, the amount of taxes shall not be increased.

Street Taxes.

SEC. 64.—To require, and it is hereby made the duty of every male resident of the city, over the age of eighteen and under the age of fifty years, to labor one day in each year upon the streets; but every person may at his option pay one dollar and fifty cents for the day he shall be so bound to labor: Provided, it be paid within five days from the time he shall be notified by the Street Supervisor. In default of payment as aforesaid, the same may be collected as other taxes.

Tax assessment.

SEC. 65.—The City Council shall have power by ordinance to regulate the form of assessment rolls, and prescribe the duties and define the powers of Assessors and Collectors   The annual assessment rolls shall be returned by the Assessor on or before the first Monday of April in each year; but the time may be extended or additions made thereto by order of the City Council. On the return thereof the City Council shall fix a day for hearing objections thereto, and any person feeling aggrieved by the assessment of his property may appear at the time specified and make his objections, which shall be heard and determined upon by the City Council; and they shall have power to alter, add to, take from and otherwise correct and revise said assessment roll.

Tax collection.

SEC. 66.—The Collector shall be furnished, within thirty days after the assessment rolls are corrected, with a list of the taxes to be collected; and if not paid, the Collector shall have power to collect said taxes with interest and cost by suit in the Corporate name, or by distress and sale of any property belonging to persons so indebted. The Assessor's roll shall in all cases be evidence on the part of the Corporation.

SEC. 67.—All taxes and assessments, general and special, Collectors. shall be collected by the Collector or Collectors in the same manner and with the same power and authority as are given by the law to Collectors of County and Territorial taxes: Provided, the Council shall have power to prescribe by city ordinance the powers, duties and liabilities of Assessors and Collectors.

SEC. 68.—The City Council shall have power to make, ordain Fire regulations. and establish all such general regulations for the prevention and extinguishment of fires, fixing of chimneys, flues and stove pipes, as they may deem expedient; to procure fire engines and other apparatus used for the extinguishment of the same, and have the charge and control of and provide, fit up and secure engine houses and other places for the keeping and preserving the same; to organize fire, hose and ladder companies, appoint foremen therefor and prescribe their duties, and make rules and regulations for their government, and to impose reasonable fines and forfeitures for a violation of the same.

SEC. 69.—The City Council shall have power to provide for School Inspectors. the election of trustees; to appoint a Board of School Inspectors and to prescribe the powers and duties of the same, and to enact such ordinances as may be necessary to carry their duties and powers into effect.

SEC. 70.—The City Council shall have exclusive authority Police. and power to establish and regulate the Police of the city; to impose fines, forfeitures and penalties for the breach of any ordinance; to provide for the recovery of such fines and forfeitures and the enforcement of such penalties, and to pass, make, ordain, establish and execute all such ordinances, not repugnant to the Constitution of the United States or the laws of this Territory, as they may deem necessary for carrying into effect and execution the powers specified in this act, and for the peace, good order, regulation, convenience and cleanliness of the city, for the protection of property therein from destruction by fire or otherwise, and for the health, safety and happiness of the inhabitants thereof.

SEC. 71.—All ordinances passed by the City Council shall, Ordinances. within one month after they shall have been passed, be published in some newspaper printed in said city, or certified copies thereof be posted up in three of the most public places in the city.

Publica-
tion.

SEC. 72.—All ordinances of the city may be proven by the seal of the Corporation, and, when printed or published in book form, purporting to be printed or published by the authority of the City Council, the same shall be received in evidence in all Courts or places without further proof.

Duties of
Officers.

SEC. 73.—The City Council shall have power, from time to time, to require further and other duties of all officers whose duties are herein provided ; and prescribe the duties and powers of all officers appointed or elected under this act, whose duties herein are not specifically mentioned, and arrange the fees and

Bonds.

fix the compensation of all officers, jurors, witnesses and others. They may also require bonds to be given to Great Salt Lake City by all officers, for the faithful performance of their duties.

Commis-
sions.

SEC. 74.—All persons appointed under this act to the office of Recorder, Marshal, Attorney, Treasurer, Collector, Assessor, Auditor of Public Accounts, Surveyor or Street Commissioner, shall be commissioned by warrant under the Corporate seal, signed by the Mayor or presiding officer of the City Council and Recorder.

City pro-
perty.

SEC. 75.—If any person, having been an officer in Great Salt Lake City, shall not, within ten days after notification and request, deliver to his successor in office all the property, papers and effects of every description in his possession belonging to said city or appertaining to the office he held, he shall forfeit and pay for the use of the city not exceeding one hundred dollars, besides all damages caused by his neglect or refusal to to deliver.

Streets.

SEC. 76.—When it shall be necessary to take private property for opening, widening or altering any public street, lane, avenue or alley, the Corporation shall make a just compensation therefor to the person whose property is so taken ; and if the amount of such compensation cannot be agreed upon, the Mayor shall cause the same to be ascertained by a jury of six disinterested men, who shall be inhabitants of the city.

Jurors.

SEC. 77.—All jurors empanneled to inquire into the amounts of benefit or damages that shall happen to the owners of property so proposed to be taken, shall first be sworn to that effect, and shall return to the Mayor or presiding officer of the City Council their inquest in writing, signed by each juror.

Cemetery

SEC. 78.—The cemetery lots which have or may hereafter be laid out and sold by said city for private places of burial shall, with their appurtenances, forever be exempt from execution or attachment.

SEC. 79.—All ordinances, resolutions and regulations now in force in Great Salt Lake City, and not inconsistent with this act, shall remain in force until altered, modified or repealed by the City Council after this act shall take effect. Old Ordinances.

SEC. 80.—All actions, rights, fines, penalties and forfeitures, in suit or otherwise, which have accrued under the ordinance incorporating Great Salt Lake City, shall be vested in and prosecuted by the Corporation hereby created. Actions continued

SEC. 81.—All plots and surveys of lands, lots or other places within said city, heretofore surveyed by the Surveyor, and all plots and surveys of lands, lots or other places that may be hereafter surveyed, and all certificates of surveys given by him shall be deemed valid by this act. Surveys validated.

SEC. 82.—All property, real, personal or mixed, now belonging to Great Salt Lake City, is hereby vested in the Corporation created by this act; and the officers of said Corporation now in office shall respectively continue in the same, until superseded in conformity to the provisions hereof, but shall be governed by this act, which shall be in force from and after its passage. Property vested. Officers continued

SEC. 83.—This act shall be deemed a public act, and may be read in evidence without proof, and judicial notice shall be taken thereof in all Courts and place. Public Act.

SEC. 84.—This act shall not invalidate any act done by the present City Council of Great Salt Lake City, or by its officers, nor divest their successors under this act of any rights, property or otherwise, or liability which may have accrued to or been created by said Council prior to the passage of this act. Rights reserved.

SEC. 85.—All officers of the city, created conservators of the peace by this act, shall have power to arrest or cause to be arrested, with or without process, all persons who shall break the peace ; commit for examination, and, if necessary, detain such persons in custody forty-eight hours in the city prison or other safe place ; and shall have and exercise such other powers, as conservators of the peace, as the City Council may prescribe. Powers of arrest.

SEC. 86.—Nothing in this act shall be so construed as to deprive the present City Council of Great Salt Lake City of any power or authority conferred upon them by the ordinance incorporating said city, and the act amendatory thereto ; but said City Council shall possess, exercise and enjoy all the powers and authority heretofore conferred upon them, except so far as such powers and authority have been expressly modified or repealed City Council.

by this act, until said City Council are superseded by the election and qualification of their successors under this act.

Acts re
pealed.

SEC. 87.—That "An ordinance to incorporate Great Salt Lake City," approved Jan. 19, 1851, be and is hereby repealed ; and "An act in relation to the assessment, collection and expenditure of a tax for road and other purposes, within incorporated cities," approved June 4, 1853, so far as the same applies to Great Salt Lake City, be and is hereby repealed.

Quarterly
statement

SEC. 88.—The City Council shall publish, in at least one newspaper published in Great Salt Lake City, a quarterly statement of the amount of city revenue, specifying in said statement from whence derived and for what disbursed.

Approved Jan. 20, 1860.

———:o:———

An ACT to amend An Act to incorporate Great Salt Lake City,
Approved Jan. 20, 1860.

Appeals.

SEC. 1.—Be it enacted by the Governor and Legislative Assembly of the Territory of Utah: That appeals shall be allowed from the Mayor and Alderman's Courts of said City to the Probate Court of Great Salt Lake County, under the same regulations and restrictions as are or may be provided for appeals from Justices of the Peace to the Probate Court.

Approved Jan. 20, 1862.

———:o:———

An ACT amending the Charter of Great Salt Lake City.

SEC. 1.—Be it enacted by the Governor and Legislative Assembly of the Territory of Utah :

First.—That the City Council of Great Salt Lake City shall

Livery
Stables

have power and authority to license, tax and regulate livery stables.

Second.—To license, tax and suppress hackmen, draymen, Hackmen.
carters, porters, omnibus drivers, cabmen, packers, carmen and
all others who may pursue like occupations, with or without
vehicles, and prescribe their compensation.

Third.—To establish, erect and control hospitals, infirmaries Hospitals.
and medical colleges; to purchase grounds for their erection and
improve and adorn the same; and license, control and regulate Physicians.
physicians and surgeons.

Fourth.—To purchase and improve suitable grounds for a House of
house of correction; to erect buildings thereon and adopt such Correction
rules and regulations for the government and punishment of
offenders therein, as said Council may from time to time deem
expedient.

Fifth.—To direct and control the location of railroad tracks Railroad
and depot grounds within the city and regulate or prohibit the tracks.
use of locomotive engines thereon, and may require the cars to be
used within the inhabited portions thereof to be drawn or pro-
pelled by other power than that of steam.

Sixth.—To regulate and control the location of gas works, Gas works
canals, telegraph poles and all improvements of similar nature.

SEC. 2.—The City Council shall have power to levy and Streets
collect on real estate (or land-claims and improvements thereon) and side-
walks.
in any district or division benefited, within the limits of said
city, a sufficient tax to defray the expense of leveling, paving,
macadamizing or planking and opening and keeping in repair
the streets and sidewalks, of constructing sewers and drains and
keeping the same in repair, and of erecting lamps and lighting
the streets in such respective districts or divisions: Provided, the
money thus raised shall be exclusively expended for such purpose
in the district where such taxes are assessed, and by such person
or persons as the City Council may appoint. The amount to be
assessed for any such improvement shall be determined by the
City Council, who shall appoint three Commissioners, reputable Commis-
citizens, to make such assessment, who shall be sworn to faithfully sioners.
and impartially execute their duties.

Before entering on their duties the Commissioners shall give Commis-
six days' notice of the time and place of meeting, to all persons sioners to
assess.
interested. The Commissioners shall assess the amount directed
by the City Council on the real estate (or land-claims and
improvements) by them deemed benefited by any such improvement, in proportion to the benefit resulting thereto.

Assessment list.

When the Commissioners shall have completed their assessment and made a correct copy thereof, they shall deliver the same to the City Recorder within thirty days after their appointment, signed by all the Commissioners.

Notice.

The City Recorder shall cause a notice to be published to all persons interested, of the completion of the assessment, and the time and place shall be designated therein when the City Council shall hear appeals and objections and correct or confirm said assessment.

Tax list

When the said assessment shall have been completed, the City Recorder shall, within ten days thereafter, make a correct tax-list, which shall be delivered to the Collector or any authorized agent appointed by the City Council, who shall collect said taxes within such time as may be prescribed by said Council.

Collections.

New Assessment.

If any assessment is set aside by order of any Court, the City Council may cause a new one to be made in like manner for the same purpose, for the collection of the amount so assessed.

Additional assessment.

If the first assessment prove insufficient, another may be made in the same manner, or, if too large a sum shall at any time be raised, the excess shall be refunded, rateably, to those by whom it was paid.

Approved Jan. 14, 1865.

————:o:————

An ACT extending the boundaries of Great Salt Lake City Corporation.

City limits extended and defined.

Be it enacted by the Governor and Legislative Assembly of the Territory of Utah: That the boundaries of Great Salt Lake City are hereby extended as follows: commencing at the northwest corner of Great Salt Lake City Corporation limits, thence west three hundred and twenty rods, thence due south to a point opposite the southern boundary of the Corporation line of Great Salt Lake City, thence east to the River Jordan; and the boundary lines of the City Corporation of Great Salt Lake City are hereby established in accordance with the provisions of this Act.

Approved Jan. 18, 1867.

An ACT changing the name of Great Salt Lake City and Great
Salt Lake County.

Be it enacted by the Governor and Legislative Assembly of
the Territory of Utah: That the name and style of Great Salt Change of
Lake City, wherever it occurs in the charter and on the corporate City title.
seal of said city and elsewhere, shall hereafter be Salt Lake City;
and that all questions, rights, property and interests pending and
accrued under the former name and style shall be continued and
deemed of the same force and virtue under the new name and
style of Salt Lake City, and that the name and style of Great
Salt Lake County, wherever it occurs in the records and on the Of County
seal of said County and elsewhere, shall hereafter be Salt Lake title.
County; and that all questions, rights, property and interests
pending and accrued under the former name and style shall be
continued and deemed of the same force and virtue under the new
name and style of Salt Lake County.

Approved Jan. 29, 1868.

————:o:————

An ACT amending the Charters of Incorporated Cities.

SEC. 1.—Be it enacted by the Governor and Legislative
Assembly of the Territory of Utah: That the Mayor and Alder- Jurisdic-
men of each incorporated city, shall be Justices of the Peace tion of
within the limits of their respective cities, and be commissioned Justices.
as such by the Governor, and shall have jurisdiction in cases
arising under the rules, laws and ordinances thereof; also in
cases arising under the laws of the Territory; and all fines,
penalties and forfeitures, collected by them, arising under the
ordinances of said city, shall be paid into the treasuries of their Fines.
respective cities; and all fines, penalties and forfeitures, collected
by them, arising under the laws of the Territory, shall be paid
into their respective County treasuries.

SEC. 2.—All cases arising under the ordinances of any city
may be commenced by affidavit and warrant issued thereon: Actions.
Provided, that any officer having probable cause to believe an offence has been committed, may arrest any supposed offender before Arrests.

B

affidavit filed or warrant issued. The affidavit shall be sufficient if it refer to the ordinance by its title and date.

Violation of ordinances.   SEC. 3.—The City Council of any city shall have power to provide by ordinance for imprisonment and forfeiture in cases of violation of city ordinance: Provided, that Justices of the Peace within and for the respective cities shall have exclusive jurisdiction in all cases of fines for crimes or misdemeanors arising under the ordinances of the city, where the fine does not exceed one hundred dollars or imprisonment not exceeding six months, or both fine and imprisonment.

Schools.   SEC. 4.—To provide for public schools or other institutions of learning, for officers and teachers, determine their powers and duties, provide for school fund by direct tax or otherwise, and how the same shall be collected and disbursed.

Fires.   SEC. 5.—The City Councils of the respective cities for the purpose of protecting property against loss by fire, may by ordinance define the limits of fire districts, and prohibit the erection of wooden buildings therein.

Licenses.   SEC. 6.—To license, tax and regulate lawyers, surgeons, physicians, dentists and other like professions, and prevent, by penalties, quacks and other pretenders.

Licenses.   SEC. 7.—To license, tax and regulate bankers, agents, expressmen, express companies, telegraphers, photographers, assayers, smelters, crushers, and other like occupations or pursuits.

Games.   SEC. 8.—The City Councils of the respective cities are hereby empowered by ordinance to prevent, punish or prohibit every kind of fraudulent device and practice and all games of hazard, and punish the keepers of houses wherein the same is conducted.

Games. *Disorderly Houses.*   SEC. 9.—To license, tax, regulate and suppress billiard tables, pin alleys, or tables and ball alleys: to repress or restrain bawdy and other disorderly houses and punish the keepers thereof.

Repeal.   SEC. 10.—So much of the city charters of the several cities as conflict with the foregoing sections of the act are hereby repealed.

   SEC. 11.—An act entitled "An act extending the boundaries *Boundaries of Salt Lake City.* of Great Salt Lake City Corporation, approved January eighteenth, eighteen hundred and sixty-seven, is hereby amended by inserting after the words River Jordan, thence northerly down the west bank of said River Jordan to a point west of the south line of Tenth South Street, thence east along said south line to the east line of the corporate limits; and so much of section one of said act as conflicts with this section is hereby repealed.

Approved Feb. 15, 1872.

CITY ORDINANCES.

CHAPTER 1.

THE CITY CHARTER TO HAVE THE FORCE AND EFFECT OF AN ORDINANCE.

SEC. 1. Be it ordained by the City Council of Salt Lake City, that the act of incorporation of said city, approved January 20, 1860, and all acts amendatory thereof, be and the same are hereby declared to have the same force and effect within the limits of said city as if the provisions thereof had been specially ordained by said council. *Declaration.*

SEC. 2. The punishment for the violation of any of the provisions of said act of incorporation, and of all acts amendatory thereof, and of all ordinances of said city when no other penalty is prescribed, shall be by fine not exceeding one hundred dollars, or by imprisonment not exceeding six months, or by both fine and imprisonment at the discretion of the court. *Penalties.*

CHAPTER II.

IN RELATION TO CITY ORDINANCES.

Repeal of ordinance not to bar proceedings.

SEC. 1. Be it ordained by the City Council of Salt Lake City that no action, cause of action, prosecution, suit, or proceeding pending at the time any ordinance or part of any ordinance shall be repealed, shall be affected in any way by such repeal, but all such actions, causes of action, prosecutions, suits, or proceedings shall proceed in all respects as if such ordinance or part of an ordinance had not been repealed.

Construction of terms.

SEC. 2. Whenever the term "heretofore" occurs in any ordinance, it shall be construed to mean any time previous to the day when such ordinance takes effect, and whenever the term "hereafter" occurs, it shall be construed to mean any time after such ordinance takes effect.

Plural to include singular.

SEC. 3. Whenever, in any ordinance or resolution, words in the plural number are used in describing or referring to any matters, parties, or persons, any single matter, party, or person, shall be deemed to be included, and *vice versa*.

SEC. 4. Whenever any subject, matter, party, or

Masculine to include feminine.

person is described or referred to in any ordinance, by words importing the singular number or the masculine gender, such words shall be deemed to include the plural

Individual to include corporations.

number and bodies-corporate as well as individuals, and females as well as males; which rule shall apply in all cases, unless it shall be otherwise expressly provided in any ordinance, or unless there be something in the subject or context repugnant to such construction.

SEC. 5. When any ordinance repealing a former Of repeals. ordinance, clause, or provision, shall itself be repealed, such repeal shall not be construed to revive such former ordinance, clause, or provision, unless it be expressly provided.

SEC. 6. If any ordinance shall be found to be in Ordinance last passconflict with or repugnant to any other ordinance, ed to be in force. that which shall have last been approved shall prevail; and so much and such parts of any prior ordinance or provision, as shall be inconsistent with such last ordinance, clause, or provision shall be deemed to be repealed thereby.

CHAPTER III.

MEETINGS OF THE CITY COUNCIL.

SEC. 1. Be it ordained by the City Council of Salt Regular Lake City, that the said council shall hold their meetings. regular sessions on the first and third Tuesday of Adjourn- every month and may hold adjourned meetings, from ed meet- ings. time to time, as business may require; and the Mayor, or any two Aldermen may call special meetings by Called meetings. notice to each of the members of said council, served personally or left at their usual place of abode.

CHAPTER IV.

REGULATING ELECTIONS.

SEC. 1. Be it ordained by the City Council of Salt Lake City, that the City election shall be held on the second Monday of February, 1874, and every two years Date of el- ection. thereafter, for one Mayor, five Aldermen, nine Coun- cilors, one Recorder, one Treasurer and one Marshal. Officers el- ected.

Qualifica-
tions of of-
ficers and
electors.
SEC. 2. No person shall be elected or appointed to any city office unless he is a citizen of the United States, and has been a constant resident of said city during at least one year next preceding such election or appointment; neither shall any person be eligible to vote at any election unless he possesses the qualifications of a voter, as prescribed by the laws of the Territory, and unless he or she is a citizen of the United States, over twenty-one years of age, and has been a constant resident in said city, during the six months next preceding said election.

Soldiers
not enti-
tled to
vote.

Exception
SEC. 3. No officer or soldier of the United States army, or other person subject to its military authority, shall be eligible to office, or entitled to vote at any municipal election in this city, unless his home or place of residence was therein at the time of engaging in such service.

Notice of
election.
SEC. 4. The City Recorder shall cause a notice of the time and places of voting and the number and kind of officers to be elected, to be posted up in five public places, or advertized in some newspaper published within said city, at least five days previous to the time of holding said election.

Judges
and Clerks
of election

Oath.

Stationery

Voting to
be by bal-
lot.
SEC. 5. The City Council shall appoint one or more Judges and one or more Clerks of election, at each place of holding elections, who shall, before entering upon their duties, take an oath for the faithful performance thereof. Said council shall furnish the necessary stationery and ballot boxes, and the voting shall be by ballot.

Voting
places.
SEC. 6. The place or places of holding said elections shall be determined by the City Council, and the polls

shall be open, to receive votes, at the hour of eight ^{Hours for voting.} o'clock in the morning and continue open until six o'clock in the evening. Each elector shall provide himself with a ballot, containing the names of the persons he wishes elected and the offices he would have them fill. When such ballot is presented, one of the ^{Mode of voting.} judges shall number and deposit it in the ballot box, and one of the clerks shall write the name of the elector opposite the number of his vote in a poll book prepared for that purpose.

SEC. 7. Any vote may be challenged by an ^{Judges to determine legality of votes.} elector, the legality of which shall be determined by the Judges; and any person casting an illegal vote at any city election, or voting, or attempting to vote twice ^{Illegal or double voting.} at the same election, shall be deemed guilty of a misdemeanor, and for each offence shall be liable to a fine ^{Penalty.} not exceeding one hundred dollars, or to imprisonment not exceeding six months, or to both fine and imprisonment.

SEC. 8. When the time for holding the election shall have expired, the judges shall seal up the ballot ^{Judges to seal and transmit ballot-boxes to City Recorder.} boxes containing the votes and the list of the names of the electors, and transmit the same within twenty-four hours to the City Recorder, who shall immediately proceed, in the presence of the Mayor or any Alderman of the City, to unseal the ballot boxes, and they shall, with such assistance as they may require, proceed to count and compare the votes with the list of names; and ^{Votes to be counted and compared.} the persons respectively receiving the highest number of votes for said offices shall be declared elected, and the Recorder shall forthwith make a brief abstract of the offices and names voted for, with the number of votes ^{Result of election to be posted.} each person received, a copy of which abstract shall be conspicuously posted at the City Hall.

Contested elections.

SEC. 9. Parties designing to contest the election of any person shall make their intention known to the City Council, by setting forth in a plain, clear, and definite manner, the grounds of contest in writing, which shall be filed with the City Recorder within three days after the abstract shall have been posted, in which case the ballots and list shall be preserved until

Ballots to be destroyed.

the contest is ended. If no notice of contest is filed within three days, the City Recorder shall destroy the

City Council to be judges of election in case of tie or contest.

ballots and list. In case of a tie of votes for two or more persons for the same office, or of a contest, the City Council shall determine which shall take his seat.

City Recorder to notify officers elect.

SEC. 10. The City Recorder shall forward to each person elected, a written notice of his election within five days thereafter, and each person so notified shall, before entering upon the duties of his office, take and

Oath of office.

subscribe an oath or affirmation that he will support the Constitution of the United States, the laws of this Territory, and the ordinances of this City, and that he will faithfully perform the duties of his office.

Mayor and Aldermen to give bonds

SEC. 11. The Mayor and Aldermen, before entering upon the duties of their respective offices shall give bonds with approved securities, each in the penal sum of ten thousand dollars to the people of Salt Lake City, conditioned for the faithful performance thereof, which shall be approved by the Recorder and filed in his office.

CHAPTER V.

CREATING CERTAIN OFFICES AND RELATING TO THE
TENURE THEREOF.

SEC. 1. Be it ordained by the City Council of Salt *Names of Officers.* Lake City, that there are hereby created the following named officers, which shall be filled by said Council, to wit:—Auditor of Public Accounts, Assessor and Collector, Supervisor of Streets, ~~Fence Viewers,~~ Captain of Police, Water Master, Sexton, Surveyor, Attorney, Inspector of Buildings, Inspector of Wood and Lumber, Sealer of Weights and Measures, ~~Inspector of Spirituous and Malt Liquors,~~ Stock Inspector, Jailor, ~~Superintendent of Insane Asylum,~~ Superintendent of Water Works, Market Masters, and Inspector of Provisions, the duties of which, together with those of the elective officers, shall be as defined by ordinance.

SEC. 2. All officers appointed by the City Council *Tenure office.* shall hold their office during the pleasure of said Council, unless otherwise provided by ordinance.

CHAPTER VI.

CITY OFFICERS.—RECORDER.

SEC. 1. Be it ordained by the City Council of Salt *Recorder to qualify.* Lake City, that the Recorder shall, before entering upon the duties of his office, take an oath of office and give bonds with approved security, to Salt Lake City, in the penal sum of five thousand dollars, conditioned for the faithful performance of the duties thereof. Said bonds shall be filed with, and approved by, the Mayor of said City.

SEC. 2. It shall be the duty of the Recorder to keep the records, papers and seal of said city, and record, in order of date, all ordinances and resolutions passed by the City Council, in a book to be kept for that purpose. He shall keep in a separate book a record of the proceedings of said Council.

Duties of Recorder.

SEC. 3. The Recorder shall pay over all money or other property belonging to the city and coming into his hands by virtue of his office, to the Treasurer or other person to whom it may be due. He shall have power to take acknowledgments, administer oaths and receive and approve bonds. He shall also have and keep a plot of all surveys within said city; and shall deliver to his successor in office the corporate seal, together with all records and proceedings of the City Council, and all books or other property in his possession, belonging to said City.

Additional duties and powers.

TREASURER.

SEC. 4. The Treasurer shall qualify and give bonds in the same manner as the Recorder; provided, that the bonds shall be in the penal sum of fifty thousand dollars, and shall be filed with the Recorder.

Treasurer to qualify and give bonds.

SEC. 5. The Treasurer shall receive all moneys belonging to the city, whether the same be raised by taxation or otherwise, and shall be the custodian of all the property of the city, the custody of which is not otherwise provided for. He shall disburse the funds and surrender the property of the city only upon orders signed by the Auditor of Public Accounts, except as hereinafter provided. He shall keep in suitable books a full account of all receipts and disbursements, with the names of persons paying or receiving such funds and the objects thereof, and shall,

Treasurer to be custodian of funds and property of City.

Books of account.

on or before the first day of December in each year <small>Annual Report.</small>
present to the City Council a full report of his receipts
and disbursements, with vouchers for all sums disbursed.

SEC. 6. The Treasurer's books of account shall be the
property of the city, and shall, together, with moneys, <small>Transfer</small>
papers or other property in his possession belonging to <small>of books, moneys</small>
the city, be delivered to his successor in office imme- <small>and property to</small>
diately after said successor shall have been duly <small>successor.</small>
elected and qualified.

MARSHAL.

SEC. 7. The Marshal shall qualify, and give bonds <small>Marshal to qualify</small>
in the same manner as the Treasurer, provided that he <small>and give bonds.</small>
shall give bonds in the penal sum of five thousand
dollars.

SEC. 8. The Marshal shall, by himself or deputies, <small>Duties and pow-</small>
attend all regular and special meetings of the City <small>ers.</small>
Council; shall have charge of the City Hall,and see that
the same is lighted and warmed when necessary; act
as doorkeeper or sergeant-at-arms; execute all orders of
the Mayor or Council; preserve the peace and good
order of the city; quell all riots, arrest and bring disorderly persons before the Mayor or Aldermen for trial,
either with or without process; serve all processes
issued by the Mayor or any Alderman to him directed
and see that all orders and judgments of said courts
are carried into effect, and shall take such measures as
shall secure the peace and good order of all public
meetings. Said Marshal may at any time call upon
the Captain of Police, or in the absence of the captain,
upon any policeman,which officers are hereby required to
assist the Marshal in maintaining the peace and good
order of the city.

May appoint Deputies.

SEC. 9. The Marshal shall have power to appoint one or more deputies as he may deem necessary, for whose official acts he shall be responsible, whose term of office shall expire with that of the Marshal, or who may be removed by him at pleasure. Said deputy or deputies shall, before acting as such, take an oath for the faithful performance of the duties of said office.

AUDITOR OF PUBLIC ACCOUNTS.

Auditor to qualify and give bonds.

SEC. 10. The Auditor of Public Accounts, shall qualify and give bonds in the same manner as the Treasurer, provided that the bond shall be in the penal sum of ten thousand dollars.

Duties.

SEC. 11. It shall be the duty of the Auditor to examine and audit all public accounts connected with the financial affairs of the city, and issue orders upon the Treasurer in liquidation of claims allowed, or appropriations made by the City Council. He shall have the

Custodian of papers.

custody of, and keep all books, papers, records, documents, vouchers, and all conveyances, leases, mortgages, bonds and other securities appertaining to the fiscal affairs of the city, which are not required by ordinance to be kept in some other office or place.

To make quarterly report.

SEC. 12. The Auditor shall make a report to the City Council quarterly, setting forth a statement of the amount of city revenue, specifying in said statement from whence derived and for what disbursed, and shall deliver to his successor in office all books, moneys, accounts, or other property in his custody belonging to the city, as soon as his successor shall be qualified.

SUPERVISOR OF STREETS.

SEC. 13. The Supervisor of Streets shall qualify and give bonds in the same manner as the Treasurer; pro-

vided that the bonds shall be in the penal sum of ten Supervisor to qualify and give bonds.
thousand dollars.

SEC. 14. The Supervisor may appoint assistant
supervisors in the various wards as he may deem neces- May appoint assistants.
sary, who shall be under his direction, and for whose
official acts he shall be responsible.

SEC. 15. It shall be the duty of the Supervisor to see Duties.
that all ordinances, or orders of the City Council, relating to streets, sidewalks and ditches, are complied
with.

SEC. 16. The Supervisor shall make a full report Supervisor to report quarterly.
quarterly, in writing, to the City Council of all things
done, and of all moneys expended in his department,
and for what purpose, and it shall also be his duty to To be custodian of certain property.
take charge of all tools or other material or property
belonging to the city and employed in working the
streets.

CAPTAIN OF POLICE AND POLICEMEN.

SEC. 17. The Captain of Police, before entering upon Captain of Police.
the duties of his office, shall take and subscribe an oath
for the faithful performance thereof, which shall be Oath of office.
filed in the office of the City Recorder.

SEC. 18. The Captain of Police shall have the direction and control of the Police, and may in any case
of breach of ordinance arrest the person or persons Duties.
offending, or report the same forthwith to the Mayor
or any Alderman, and shall be under the direction of
the Mayor in maintaining the peace and good order of
the city. He shall report quarterly, or oftener if re- To report.
quired, in writing to the City Council, a true and
certified account of the number of arrests, and class

of crimes that have come within his knowledge, and
also the amount of service performed by each policeman.

Police-
men to be
appointed
by Mayor.

SEC. 19. The Mayor is hereby authorized to appoint,
or employ any number of Policemen which, in his
judgment, the exigency of the times requires; he
shall assign them their duties, and shall have power to
control and direct them in the discharge thereof.

Police reg-
ulations
provided
for.

SEC. 20. The Mayor and Captain of Police are authorized and required to make all needful rules and
regulations, not inconsistent with the ordinances of the
city, for the government and control of the police
department.

Police-
men to
take oath
of office.

SEC. 21. Every Policeman appointed shall take an
oath for the faithful performance of his duties as policeman, and shall see that the ordinances of the city are
complied with; they shall also watch the conduct of

Duties.

persons of known or suspected bad character, and
shall report such persons to the Captain of Police,
whose duty it shall be to report to the Mayor without
delay.

Powers.

SEC. 22. Any Policeman may arrest and bring offenders before the Mayor or Aldermen, with or without process, and shall be subject to the orders and
directions of the Captain of Police.

WATER MASTER.

Water
Master to
qualify.

SEC. 23. The Water Master shall qualify in the same
manner as the Treasurer, provided that no bond shall
be exacted of him unless specially ordered by the City

Duties.

Council. It shall be his duty to see to the erection and
repairs of such gates, locks, dams, or sluices as may
be necessary to regulate within the city the waters

flowing therein, and divide the same through the city as shall best serve the public interest, for irrigation, domestic and other purposes.

SEC. 24. It shall be the duty of the City Water Master to appoint one or more assistant water masters *Assistants* in each of the bishops' wards of the city, who shall act under his direction, and the assistant water masters shall distribute the water to the inhabitants of their respective wards, in such a manner as they may deem necessary and just.

SEC. 25. Any person or persons who shall remove, *Penalties* break, or otherwise injure or destroy any lock, dam, *for injuries.* gate or sluiceway, shall be liable to a fine of not less than one nor more than one hundred dollars.

SEC. 26. Any person or persons who shall take, or *Penalties* alter the course of, the water intended for irrigation or *for altering water* other purposes, without the consent of the Water *courses.* Master, or the person then holding the right of said water, shall be liable to a fine of not less than one, nor more than fifty dollars for every such offence.

SEC. 27. It shall be the duty of the inhabitants of each bishops' ward to make and keep in repair such *Inhabitants to* locks, dams, gates, or sluiceways as may be necessary *keep water* to secure an equal and fair distribution of water to the *courses, etc., in repair.* several wards, the same to be under the control of the Water Master in each ward.

SEC. 28. It shall be the duty of the Water Master to *Water* adjudicate all difficulties arising from the distribution *Master to adjudicate* of water in the several wards. *difficulties*

SEC. 29. It shall also be the duty of the Water Master *To report.* to report quarterly his proceedings to the City Council, commencing on the first Tuesdays of March, June, September and December of each year, and to recommend such improvements as he may deem necessary for their action.

SEXTON AND BURYING GROUNDS.

Sexton to qualify and give bonds.

SEC. 30. The Sexton shall qualify and give bonds in the same manner as the Treasurer, provided that the bonds shall be in the penal sum of five hundred dollars.

Duties.

SEC. 31. It shall be the duty of the Sexton to take charge of the public burying grounds in Salt Lake City; to see to the digging of graves, furnishing of coffins, and conveying the dead when called upon so to do by any persons entitled to bury in said grounds; and to keep a record of all deaths of persons buried in said burying grounds which shall come under his observation, or shall be reported to him by the citizens of said city, which record shall include the name of the person deceased, with his or her parent's names; where and when born; the time of death and the cause thereof; together with the name of the physician or nurse who attended such person.

Sexton may sell lots.

To report sales and pay over moneys.

shall give certificate of sale.

SEC. 32. The Sexton is hereby authorized to sell lots in said grounds and to collect all dues arising from such sales; and all such sales shall be reported by him to the Treasurer; and all moneys received by him therefor, less ten per cent. which shall be retained by him as a commission, shall be paid into the City Treasury as often as once in three months. He shall give to each purchaser a certificate of payment therefor, with a description of the lot or lots so purchased. And the Mayor of said city is hereby authorized to make to said purchaser, a good and sufficient title to _{Mayor to give title.} said lot or lots, on presentation to him of said certifi-_{Price of lots.} cate. The price of each of said lots shall not exceed the sum of twelve dollars, and all lots or parts of lots _{Lots exempt from taxation and execution.} thus conveyed, together with all improvements thereon, shall be exempt from taxation and execution.

Sec. 33. The Sexton is hereby authorized to collect from those requiring his services, not more than the following compensation:

_{Compensation.}

For furnishing and staining a plain coffin, per
    foot, running measure,   -   -   -   - $1.25
For digging grave four feet in length and under,   2.00
For all graves over four feet in length,   -   3.00
   All graves shall be not less than six feet in depth, and the above prices shall include the replacing of the earth in all graves dug by said Sexton.
For conveying coffin to any part of the city, per
    mile or fractional part thereof,   -   -   -   50c.
For conveying the dead from any part of said
    city to the burying ground in the city hearse, $2.50
For recording, as required in this ordinance,   25c.

Sec. 34. The Sexton is hereby authorized to appoint _{Sexton to appoint Porter.} a Porter for the cemetery, subject to the approval of the council. It shall be the duty of said Porter to dig _{Duties.} graves and to take charge of and improve the cemetery grounds under the direction of the Sexton, for which service he shall be compensated at the rate of _{Fees.} two dollars per day; and if the number of graves dug by him is not sufficient at the aforesaid rates to pay said sum, then the city shall pay any deficiency which may arise.

Sec. 35. The owners of lots, or the relatives or friends
c

Owners to designate location of lots and graves.

of deceased persons buried in said grounds, are hereby required to erect bounds or monuments at the corners of their lots, or head boards with the names of the deceased thereon, indicating the lot or grave of persons

To report same to Sexton.

so buried, and to report the same, together with the information required, to the Sexton; and if any person fails to erect such bounds, monument or board, it shall be done by the Sexton at the expense of the person owning or burying in such lot.

Burials to be confined to burying grounds.

SEC. 36. No person or persons, shall be allowed to inter their dead within the limits of this city except in the public burying ground, unless by permission of the City Council; and no person shall bury in said

Permission to bury to be obtained.

grounds, without first obtaining title to the lot on which they bury, or permission of the person owning the lot if sold, or of the Sexton if unsold.

Sexton to direct disinterments.

SEC. 37. No person shall disinter any body buried in said grounds, except under the direction of the

Injury to grounds not allowed.

Sexton; or shall injure any monument, shrub, tree, or any other property belonging to said grounds or being thereon.

Burial of murderers in City Cemetery prohibited.

SEC. 38. There shall not be interred within the limits of the cemetery of said city, the body of any person known to the law as a murderer; and any person vio-

Penalties for violation of this ordinance.

lating any provision of this subdivision or this ordinance, shall be liable to a fine, in any sum not exceeding one hundred dollars, or to imprisonment for any term not exceeding six months or to both fine and imprisonment.

INSPECTOR OF BUILDINGS.

SEC. 39. The Inspector of Buildings, before entering upon the duties of his office, shall take and subscribe an oath for the faithful performance thereof, which Oath of office. shall be filed in the office of the City Recorder.

SEC. 40. It shall be the duty of the Inspector of To inspect buildings Buildings, when called upon, to examine all public or and ma- private buildings, bridges, dams, locks, gates, reser- terials. voirs, aqueducts, or other public works, and certify as to the strength, safety, workmanship and general condition of the same. He shall also, when requested, inspect all building material which may be offered for sale, measure all buildings, building material, mason and other mechanical work, and, when required, certify to the measurement thereof, which certificate shall be evidence of the things therein certified.

SEC. 41. Said Inspector shall, when he may deem it necessary, carefully inspect buildings in the course of construction, and shall cause to be carried into effect To enforce ordin- all ordinances providing for the prevention of fires; and ances. he may require the removal, or prevent the construction of any fire-place, chimney, hearth, stove, or pipe' in any building which may seem to endanger life or property, and may direct the construction of safe places of deposit for ashes; and may require the removal of all shavings, straw, packing, papers, or other rubbish from back-yards, buildings or other places, by the owners or occupants thereof; and for all such service Compen- sation. he shall be paid a reasonable compensation by the parties requiring such service, or in behalf of whose property the same shall be rendered.

SEC. 42. Any person who shall neglect or refuse to conform to the provisions of this ordinance or the in- Penalty. structions of said Inspector as herein provided, after having been served with a notice in writing setting forth distinctly some one of the dangers hereinbefore stated, with instructions to remedy the same without delay, shall be liable, for each offence, to a fine in any sum not exceeding one hundred dollars.

SEALER OF WEIGHTS AND MEASURES.

Sealer to qualify and give bonds. SEC. 43. The Sealer of Weights and Measures shall qualify and give bonds in the same manner as the Treasurer; provided that the bonds be in the penal sum of one thousand dollars.

Weights and measures to be examined and tested.

To be stamped.

Certificate of accuracy to be given. SEC. 44. The Sealer of Weights and Measures shall, twice every year, at intervals not exceeding six months, and oftener if required, examine and test the accuracy of all weights, measures, scales, or other things used by merchants and others for weighing or measuring anything bought or sold by them; he shall stamp with a suitable seal, to be prescribed by the Mayor, all weights, measures and scales so used, which he may find conformed to, or which he may cause to conform to, the standard prescribed by the laws of this Territory, and shall deliver to the owner thereof a certificate of the accuracy of such weights and measures as shall be found to be or shall be rendered correct.

Register to be kept.

False measures etc., to be seized.

Report to be made. SEC. 45. It shall further be his duty to register the names of all persons whose weights, measures or scales he may find to be accurate or may cause to be rendered accurate, and of all persons who fail to have the same corrected when found incorrect. He shall seize in the name of the city all false weights, measures and scales which he may find, and which the owner shall fail to have made comformable to the provision of this ordinance without delay, and shall immediately report such persons to the Mayor or Aldermen; he shall also further report in writing every six months to the City

Recorder the names of the owners and the number of weights, measures and scales examined and found by him to be correct.

SEC. 46. All persons using weights,measures,scales, or other things for weighing or measuring any article bought or sold in this city, shall cause the same to be examined, tested and sealed as hereinbefore provided, and any person failing so to do shall be liable to pay a fine of not less than one nor more than fifty dollars for each offence. *Persons using weights, measures, etc., must cause the same to be inspected.*

Penalty.

SEC. 47. The Sealer of Weights and Measures shall be entitled to receive for each examination, testing, sealing and certifying, as hereinbefore required, the following fees, which shall be collected from the owner or owners of the weights, measures, scales or other article inspected: *Fees of Sealer.*

Any steelyards, or beam, ground, floor, platform, counter, or other scales by which may be weighed not exceeding two hundred pounds,	25c.
Any such instrument by which may be weighed over two hundred and less than six hundred pounds, - - - -	50c.
Over six hundred and less than twelve hundred pounds, - - - -	$1.00
Over twelve hundred pounds, - -	1.50
For any yard stick, dry or liquor measure,	10c.
Any nest or set of measures, - -	25c.

And the weights attached to any scale shall, as to the compensation of the Sealer of Weights and Measures be considered a part of the scale; provided that where any such weight, measure or instrument. previously inspected, shall, upon subsequent examination, be found correct, and shall not be required to be stamped a second time, the aforesaid Sealer of Weights and Measures shall not receive more than one-half the compensation provided for.

Sealer to inspect when required.

SEC. 48. The Sealer of Weight sand Measures shall examine and test any of the before-mentioned instruments for weighing or measuring, on application by any person who shall tender to him the fee which, by the preceding section, he is authorized to receive, and he shall, in every case where he may employ labor or material in making accurate any weight or measure, be entitled to extra compensation therefor, and to retain the article upon which such labor or material has been employed until such compensation be paid.

Extra compensation.

Deputies.

SEC. 49. The said Sealer of Weights and Measures may appoint one or more deputies, subject to the approval of the City Council, and such deputies shall qualify in like manner and perform the same duties and be entitled to the same fees as is herein provided for the Sealer of Weights and Measures.

INSPECTOR OF LIQUORS.

Inspector shall qualify and give bonds

SEC. 50. The Inspector of Liquors shall, before entering on the duties of his office, qualify, in the same manner as the City Treasurer, provided, that the bonds shall be in the sum of five hundred dollars.

Liquors in bulk to be inspected.

SEC. 51. All spirituous liquors, received, stored or vended within the limits of said city, shall be inspected by the Inspector of Liquors before the same are offered for sale, except such as are brought into said city in bottles.

SEC. 52. It shall be the duty of said Inspector to *U.S. proof standard adopted.* inspect all liquors which may be subject to inspection, according to the proof standard established by the United States, and to mark with paint on the barrel or vessel containing such liquor, the quantity and *Marks.* strength thereof, the date of inspection, and the name of the Inspector.

SEC. 53. It shall be the duty of said Inspector to *Duty of Inspector.* inspect all liquors within the limits of said city, and guage all casks or other vessels containing such liquors, when called on for such purpose, and said Inspector shall be entitled to receive from the person requiring such service the following prescribed fees, to wit:

Fees.

For inspecting one cask or vessel of liquor, - $1.00
For all over one cask or vessel, in the same lot,
   and not exceeding ten casks, each, - 50c.
For all over ten casks in the same lot, each, 25c.
For guaging one cask or vessel, - - 1.00
For guaging all over one cask or vessel, and not
   over five, each, - - - - 50c.
For guaging all over five, each, - - 25c.

SEC. 54. All such spirituous liquors offered for *Liquors subject to inspection at any time.* sale within said city shall be liable to inspection or re-inspection, at any time; but the owner thereof shall not be liable to pay for more than one inspection of the *Fees to paid but once.* same lot of liquor. And no person shall alter, change, or deface the Inspector's marks on any barrel, cask, or other vessel containing liquors so inspected and offered *Prohibition.* for sale, or shall reduce in strength, or adulterate the same.

SEC. 55. It shall be the duty of said Inspector to *Reports.* make to the City Recorder of said city, annually, or oftener if required by said Council, a report of the quantity, kind and strength of liquors inspected by him, and the names of the persons offering such liquors for sale. He shall also make report forthwith, to the Mayor or any Alderman of said city, of any and all liquors which he may find adulterated, or changed from the proof marked on said casks or vessels, as hereinbefore required.

Penalties.   SEC. 56. Any person violating the provisions of this subdivision shall be liable to a fine in any sum not exceeding one hundred dollars for each offence, or to imprisonment not exceeding six months, or to both fine and imprisonment.

INSPECTOR OF PROVISIONS.

Official Oath.   SEC. 57. The Inspector of Provisions shall, before entering upon the duties of his office, take and subscribe an oath for the faithful performance thereof, which shall be filed with the City Recorder.

Duties.   SEC. 58. It shall be the duty of said Inspector, when requested, to inspect all meats, flour, vegetables, or other provisions, and certify to the quality of the Compensation. same, for which he shall be entitled to a reasonable compensation from the person requiring such service.

SEC. 59. It shall further be his duty, when provisions are offered for sale, and he may deem it necessary for the health and protection of the citizens, to inspect the same, and should any be found unfit to Power of seizure. offer to the public, he is hereby authorized to seize, in the name of the city, and hold such provisions, subject to the direction of the Mayor or Alderman before whom the person so offending shall be brought; and said person, upon conviction shall be liable to a fine of not less than one nor more than one hundred dollars, and shall be further liable to forfeit said provisions to the City, at the discretion of the Court. *Penalty for offering unwholesome provisions.*

SEC. 60. Said Inspector shall make report of his proceedings quarterly in writing to the City Council. *To report.*

STOCK INSPECTOR.

SEC. 61. The Stock Inspector shall qualify in the same manner as the Treasurer, and give bonds in a like sum. *Inspector to qualify.*

SEC. 62. It shall be the duty of said Inspector to take charge of the city stock-market, and to receive all stock that shall be brought thereto for sale or inspection. *Inspector to take charge of market.* He shall also keep a book, in which he shall record a true description, including marks and brands, of all stock inspected by him, and the names of persons bringing such stock to said market for sale or inspection. *To keep record.* Said Inspector shall be entitled to receive as compensation from any person requiring a certificate of inspection, the sum of twenty-five cents for the first, *Compensation.* and ten cents for each additional animal inspected and certified to. He shall, as often as once in three months, and oftener if required by the City Council, submit to the Treasurer a full report of all business done and *To report and pay to city moiety of funds.* moneys received as Inspector, and shall, at such periods, pay into the Treasury an equal half part of all moneys so received.

SEC. 63. All persons are hereby forbidden to sell, or offer for sale, any beef-cattle in any street, lane, alley or other public place within the limits of said city, without first having the same inspected by the Stock *Prohibition.*

Penalty. Inspector, and any person so offending shall be liable to a fine in any sum not exceeding one hundred dollars for each offence.

Beeves for slaughter to be inspected.   SEC. 64. All butchers, or other persons keeping a slaughterhouse within the limits of said city, shall obtain from said Stock Inspector a certificate of inspection of all beeves slaughtered by them, before the same shall have been slaughtered; and any butcher or slaughterman who shall kill animals for beef without first obtaining such certificate, shall be deemed guilty Penalty. of a misdemeanor, and shall be liable to a fine in any sum not exceeding one hundred dollars for each offence.

Animals offered for sale to be first inspected.   SEC. 65. All persons having license to sell horses, mules or cattle, at public or private sale, shall, before offering such animals for sale, have them inspected by the Stock Inspector, who shall record a general description of the same, including marks and brands; and if any animal so offered for inspection or sale shall have Branded animals not in owners' hands to be reported.   any recorded mark or brand of any resident of Utah Territory, and shall not be in possession of the owner of such mark or brand, it shall be the duty of said Inspector to immediately report the facts of such case to some police officer.

Penalty.   SEC. 66. Any person neglecting or refusing to comply with the provisions of this subdivision shall be liable to a fine in any sum not exceeding one hundred dollars for each offence.

JAILOR.

To qualify   SEC. 67. The Jailor shall qualify and give bonds in the same manner as the Treasurer; provided that the bonds shall be in the penal sum of five thousand dollars. *Bonds.*

SEC. 68. It shall be the duty of the Jailor to take charge of the City Prison, to cause the same to be warmed and lighted when it shall be necessary, and kept clean and in proper order. He shall have the custody of the inmates thereof, and shall see to feeding and otherwise caring for the same. He shall further- *Duties.* *Shall en-* more see that all rules prescribed by the City Council *force rules.* for the government of the prison are carried into effect.

MARKETS AND MARKET MASTERS.

SEC. 69. The said city is hereby divided into market districts, corresponding in number and limits with the municipal wards thereof. *Municipal wards de- clared market districts.*

SEC. 70. There shall be established a market, house and grounds in each district, at such time and place as shall be determined upon by the City Council and they shall be under the direction of such Market Masters as said Council may appoint. *Markets authoriz- ed.*

SEC. 71. The Market Masters in their respective districts shall have authority, and it is hereby made their duty, to make all needful rules and regulations touching the designation and arrangement of vegetable and fruit stands, and arrangement, stationing and re- moval of all wagons, carts, and other vehicles used or brought by marketers within the boundaries or limits set apart for public market purposes; provided, that such rules and regulations shall be approved by the City Council, and posted up in conspicuous places in each market house. *Market masters to make rules.* *Provision.*

To lease
stalls and
stands.
SEC. 72. The stalls and stands in the market house and grounds shall be leased by the respective Market Masters at such prices and on such terms as may be fixed from time to time, under the general direction of the City Council.

Lessee to
furnish
sureties.
SEC. 73. Each lessee of a stall or stand shall provide two or more sureties to be approved by the Market Master, who shall be jointly bound with the lessee for the payment of the rent of the stall or stand quarterly Not to
transfer
lease. in advance, and no lease shall be transferable, nor shall any other party occupy said stand or stall, except by permission of the Market Master.

Butchers'
stalls to be
painted.
SEC. 74. The lessees of the butcher's stalls shall each cause his stall to be painted or whitewashed in the months of April and October in each year.

Duties of
Market
master.
SEC. 75. It shall be the duty of the Market Masters to exercise a general supervision over their respective market house and market places, and to enforce all regulations established for the government thereof; to assign place for wagons or persons attend- To examine ar-
ticles. ing the markets, and enforce order; to examine the quality of all articles offered for sale in the markets, and to seize all blown, unsound, diseased, impure or May
seize. unwholesome articles exposed for sale, and destroy the same; to examine the weight of articles exposed for sale, and seize all which are of less weight than that Forfeit. represented by the seller, which shall be forfeited and sold for the benefit of the city, by public outcry in the market.

Master to
decide dis-
putes.
SEC. 76. Said Market Masters shall decide all disputes which may arise between buyer and seller touching the weight or measure of any article, and

shall keep suitable measures and scales or other implements for weighing, and shall be paid a reasonable fee by any party requiring such service, and shall pay over to the City Treasurer weekly, all such fees and other moneys received by them on account of the City.

SEC. 77. The Market Masters are hereby invested Power absolute. with full power and authority in all other matters connected with the markets and market places, and all persons are required to obey the rules and regulations of said markets, and the directions of said Masters therein.

SEC. 78. The Market Masters shall superintend Cleansing the cleaning of the markets and the market grounds, and shall require the occupants to sprinkle the same with water whenever it shall be necessary, to prevent and lay the dust. No provisions or other things shall be sold in the market except during market hours, Prohibition. without the permission of the Market Master, who shall be provided with a bell, and shall announce by the ringing thereof, the closing of the market house, at Closing. least ten minutes before the time of closing.

SEC. 79. The markets shall be kept open from dawn until twelve o'clock meridian of each day, except Market hours. Sunday; provided, that on general holidays they may be closed at eight o'clock a. m. and may be opened from twelve o'clock to eight o'clock in the evening of each day, Sundays excepted, by order of the City Council, when it shall be deemed necessary.

SEC. 80. Every lessee or occupant of a stall or Duties of Lessee. stand, shall, within thirty minutes after the ringing of the bell as aforesaid, cause his wagon, vehicle, or other obstruction to be removed from the market place, and his stall or stand to be thoroughly cleaned, and all animal and vegetable offal and rubbish to be removed from the houses and places, and each butcher shall cause his tables, meat blocks and other fixtures to be thoroughly scraped and cleaned.

Of dis-
eased food   SEC. 81. No person shall expose, or offer for sale, in the market, or any other place within this city, any sick or diseased live animal, usually eaten for food, for the purpose, and with the design, that the same shall be used for food; or the flesh of any dead animal which was sick, overheated or run down by dogs, or otherwise, at or before the time the same was butchered or slain, or which came to its death by any other means than the usual manner of slaying animals
Unwhole-
some food.   for food, or the flesh of any bull, boar, ram, dog, cat, or animal not commonly deemed wholesome for food,
Penalty.   under penalty of fine, not exceeding one hundred dollars, or imprisonment not exceeding six months, or both fine and imprisonment.

SEC. 82. No person shall kill or slaughter any
Other of-
fences.   animal in or about the markets, or throw or deposit any animal or vegetable offal, filth, or any other noisome substance, nor bring, nor suffer to come with him into or about the market place during market hours, any dog, bitch, or any dangerous or unruly animal.

Live ani-
mals to be
confined.   SEC. 83. No person shall expose, or offer for sale, in or about the market, any horse, cow, ox, mule, jack, hog, or other live animal, unless confined, or in a wagon, except at such place as the Market Master may direct.

SEC. 84. If the lessee of any stall or stand fail for six consecutive days to expose for sale at his stand or stall, articles usually sold thereat, unless said fail- Lease may be forfeit-ed. ure be caused by sickness or other unavoidable cir-cumstances, his lease shall be forfeited, and his stall or stand may be leased to another.

Sec. 85. If any lessee of any stall or stand be Violation of ordin-ances. Penalty. twice convicted of violating any ordinance in relation to markets, his lease on the second conviction may be adjudged forfeited.

Sec. 86. No person shall expose or offer for sale Regula-tions. at any other place than the market houses, or at his licensed place of business, any fresh meat in less quan-tities than one quarter.

Sec. 87. It shall be unlawful for any person Idlers,etc., prohibited having no business to idly sit, lounge, stand, walk or lie in or about the market house, or to bring or show any jack or stud-horse in the market grounds.

Sec. 88. All places licensed for the sale of fresh meat shall be subject to the regulations prescribed by Licenses. this subdivision so far as the same may be applicable.

Sec. 89. Any person violating the provisions of this subdivision for which no penalty is provided, or the Penalty. public rules, or orders of the Market Masters, shall be liable to a fine in any sum not exceeding twenty-five dollars for each offence.

CITY SURVEYOR.

Sec. 90. The City Surveyor shall qualify and Shall qualify and give bonds. give bonds in the same manner as the Treasurer, provided that the bonds shall be in the sum of five thousand dollars.

Initial point of city surveys defined.

SEC. 91. The point of intersection of the base and meridian lines as established by the United States survey, Salt Lake meridian, shall be the initial point of all surveys within said city, and all surveys shall conform to the original survey, as near as may be.

Duplicate plats of surveys to be filed.

SEC. 92. It shall be the duty of the City Surveyor to make a duplicate plat of the surveys and subdivisions of all property surveyed and subdivided within the limits of Salt Lake City, and file the same in the City Recorder's office, and all errors and discrepancies in original surveys or re-surveys shall be noted and filed in like manner, as soon as determined, and such duplicate plats are hereby declared to be official plats of said city.

Metes and bounds to be defined by surveyor.

SEC. 93. It shall be the duty of the City Surveyor to determine the corner or boundary lines of any block, lot or part of a lot within said city when required by any person so to do, and furnish such person a certificate of such survey when required; provided that the lawful fees are tendered him for such service.

Further duties of Surveyor.

SEC. 94. It shall be the duty of such Surveyor to determine the lines and grades of all public streets, alleys and sidewalks within the limits of said city under the direction and subject to the approval of the City Council, and to file in the office of the City Recorder a profile of all grades so determined and established, and to perform such other and further service, under the direction of, and as may be required by, the Mayor of said city.

Fees.

SEC. 95. The fees of said Surveyor shall be for all services rendered as herein required, not exceeding eight dollars per day.

ASSESSOR AND COLLECTOR.

SEC. 96. An Assessor and Collector shall be ap- Appointpointed by the City Council, whose term of office shall ment.
be one year, or until his successor is appointed
and qualified; who, before entering upon his office,
shall qualify and give bonds, in the penal sum of Bonds.
twenty thousand dollars, to the people of said city,
conditioned for the faithful performance of the duties
thereof; which bonds shall be approved by the City
Recorder and filed in his office.

SEC. 97. The Assessor and Collector is hereby em- Powers.
powered to administer oaths in the discharge of his
official duties, and may require persons to give a
statement of their taxable property under oath, and he
is hereby authorized, when necessary, to appoint one
or more deputies, for whose official acts he shall be re- Deputies.
sponsible; and they shall qualify and give bonds with
good and sufficient securities to said Assessor and
Collector, to be approved by and filed with the City
Recorder.

SEC. 98. It shall be the duty of the Assessor and Duties.
Collector to assess all property, real and personal, of
every name and nature, within the limits of this city,
not exempt by law, at its fair cash value, including
money and funds of every description, between the
first day of January, and the first Monday of April of
each year, and make returns thereof to the City Council, on or before the last mentioned date; *provided*,
that the time may be extended, and additions made to
the assessment, by order of the City Council.

SEC. 99. All goods or other property brought into Assessments.
this city by transient traders, shall be assessed, and the

D

tax collected when they are offered or exposed for sale; and any person or persons dissatisfied with their assessment may petition the City Council to have the same adjusted.

Books. SEC. 100. The Assessor may provide himself with suitable books, at the expense of the city; and shall make his residents' assessment list in alphabetical order, giving a description of all property assessed, adding thereto, under the head of unknown, all the real and personal estate within said city, not included in the assessment list of residents: *Provided*, that the **Provisions** real estate shall be described by the number of lot or portion thereof, and block and name of plat. He may, when necessary, leave with the person to be assessed, or at his residence, or place of business, a copy of the blank form of the assessment list, requiring him to fill and return the same to the Assessor within ten days; and any person furnished with said blank form must comply with the requirements, or be liable to a fine not exceeding one hundred dollars.

Assessments corrected. SEC. 101. If the Assessor shall discover any property which has not been assessed in some previous year, and which was liable to such assessment, the same shall be assessed for each year in which it was not assessed, at the value thereof, when the same should have been assessed, and the Assessor shall note the same upon his books.

Complaints. SEC. 102. On the return of the assessment roll, the City Council shall appoint a time to hear complaints (if any), and determine the Assessor and Collector's compensation; also determine the rate per cent. of the City Tax for the current year, which shall not exceed five mills on the dollar to defray the contingent expenses of the city; also, not to exceed five mills on the dollar to open, improve and keep in repair the streets of the city; and not to exceed one-and-a-quarter mills on the dollar to control the waters of said city; and they shall annually apportion and apply said taxes as shall in their judgment be deemed most expedient. Taxes.

SEC. 103. The Recorder shall, within twenty days after receiving the assessment list, set the amount of tax in the proper column, opposite the description of property, and furnish the Assessor and Collector with a correct copy of said list, with the amount of tax affixed to each name, or description of property, and file the orignal list with the office records. Duty of Recorder

SEC. 104. When the Assessor and Collector receives the tax list, he shall immediately proceed to collect the tax, and pay the amount collected into the City Treasury, monthly, or oftener if required; and shall, on or before the thirty-first day of December in each year, make a full report to, and settlement with, the City Auditor. Collections. Report.

SEC. 105. It shall be the duty of the Auditor to keep an account with the Assessor and Collector, debiting him with the amount of tax assessed, and crediting him with the amount paid into the City Treasury, the amount remitted, and compensation allowed him for his services. Accounts

SEC. 106. The Assessor and Collector shall furnish to each tax-payer, or leave at his usual place of residence or business (if known), a written notice of the amount of tax assessed against him and where payable. In case any person neglects or refuses to pay his tax within twenty days from the date of said notice, the Written notice.

52

Assessor and Collector is authorized and empowered to

Sale. take and sell, at public sale, enough taxable property belonging to the delinquent to pay his tax, with cost of collection, advertising sale and recording; giving not less than ten days' public notice of the time, place of sale and kind of property to be sold : *Provided*, the property of non-residents, or of persons unknown,

Publica- shall not be sold for taxes, without giving five inser-
tion. tions in some newspaper published and having general circulation throughout the city and County of Salt Lake, commencing twenty days previous to the date of sale.

SEC. 107. All assessments for taxes, made under

Taxes
liens upon this ordinance, shall be a lien upon the property
property. assessed from the time of the assessment, until the taxes are paid, together with costs of collection; and no sale or transfer of such property shall affect the lien.

SEC. 108. In case of the sale of real estate, the Col-

Sales of lector shall issue a certificate to the purchaser, reciting:
Real Es- —That, whereas the city taxes assessed on said
tate by
Collector. property (describing the same) remain unpaid, as appears upon the books of the Collector, and said real estate having been duly advertised for sale, in conform- ity to the ordinance of the city, in such case made and provided; therefore, the real estate was sold at public auction to the purchaser, (naming him) for the amount of said taxes and costs, giving the date of the sale and in what papers published, and acknowledging the receipt of the amount paid by the purchaser.

SEC. 109. If, at such public sale, no person bid and pay the Collector the amount required to be paid, as

Certificate aforesaid, on any real estate, the Collector shall make
to issue to
City. to the Mayor, for and in behalf of said city, a certifi-

cate, similar to that given to other purchasers, embracing, in one certificate, all such property in the city, offered for sale at public auction, as aforesaid; and such sale to the city shall have the same effect as if made to an individual.

SEC. 110. Said certificate to the city shall be delivered to the City Recorder, who shall keep the same in his office, and credit the Collector with the amount of tax assessed thereon; and within twenty days after any such sale, the Collector shall make out, in duplicate, a minute and specific report, or statement, of the sales made by him; one copy of which he shall cause to be recorded in the Recorder's office of Salt Lake County, and the other to be filed with the City Recorder, who shall record the same in a suitable book, for the inspection of all persons interested. *Certificate to be delivered.*

SEC. 111. Real estate sold for taxes, as aforesaid, may be redeemed by any person interested therein, at anytime within two years after the date of the sale thereof, by such person paying to the City Treasurer, for the use of the purchaser, or his legal representatives, the amount paid by such purchaser, and all costs, as aforesaid, with interest, at the rate of twenty-five per cent. per annum, on the whole, from the day of sale to that of the redemption, and all taxes that have accrued thereon and are unpaid at the time of the redemption, or which have been paid thereon by the purchaser after his purchase. *Redemption of property.*

SEC. 112. Money paid into the Treasury in redemption of real estate, published at a tax sale, and to which money such purchaser, or his assignee, is entitled, shall be paid to him by the Treasurer upon his apply- *Redemption funds.*

ing therefor and producing the Collector's certificate of the purchase, and endorsing thereon a receipt for the amount.

Deeds for property sold for taxes.

SEC. 113. If any property sold, as aforesaid, be not redeemed within the time, and in the manner aforesaid, on presentation of the Collector's certificate, the Recorder shall make out and deliver a deed therefor, conveying the same to the individual purchaser, or his assignee, or to the city, as the case may be; which deed shall recite, substantially, the amount of the tax, the year for which it was assessed, the day and year of the sale, the amount for which the real estate was sold, a full description thereof, and the name of the purchaser or assignee.

Taxes of transient persons.

SEC. 114. The Assessor and Collector is required and empowered to collect taxes, at the rate of the previous year, from any person he presumes will remove from the city before the regular time for collection, and to assess any person or property omitted during the time for assessments, and must report his doing under this section in the same manner as though done within the regular time.

CITY ATTORNEY.

To qualify.

SEC. 115. The City Attorney shall be appointed by the City Council, and before entering upon the duties of his office, shall take and subscribe an oath, and give bonds in the penal sum of five thousand dollars conditioned for the faithful performance thereof, which shall

Deputy.

be approved by the Mayor, and filed in the office of the City Recorder; and he may, with the approval of the Mayor, appoint a deputy, who shall take the oath of office, perform the same duties, and for whose acts the City Attorney shall be responsible.

SEC. 116.   It shall be the duty of the City Attorney to prosecute and defend in all courts in all actions on behalf of said city; and defend in all actions against any officer or agent of the city, on account of official acts. **Duties.**

SEC. 117.   To take appeals or sue out writs of error on behalf of the city or any officer as aforesaid, with the consent and approval of the Mayor, and make the necessary affidavits, and execute the necessary bonds in the name of said city. **Duties.**

SEC. 118.   To advise the City Council or their committees, or any city officer, on such legal questions as may arise in relation to the business of the city. **Duties.**

SEC. 119.   The City Attorney, having personal knowledge of any violation of a city ordinance, or upon receiving reliable information of any such violation, shall immediately institute the necessary steps to bring the offender to punishment. **Duties.**

SEC. 120.   He shall keep a record showing all claims placed in his hands for collection, all moneys received by him on account of the city, and all payments made by him to the City Treasurer, and also keep a docket-book, in which he shall enter an abstract of suits pending in any court, and judgments in favor of, or against, said city. He shall, at the end of each quarter, or oftener if required, settle with the Auditor of Public Accounts, and pay to the City Treasurer all moneys in his hands belonging to the city. **Record.** **Docket.** **Settlements.**

SEC. 121. The City Attorney shall report quarterly, **Reports.** or oftener if required, to the City Council the condition **Compensation.** of the business of the City in his hands or control, and for all services rendered as herein required, such compensation shall be allowed as shall be determined by the City Council.

QUALIFICATIONS AND REMOVALS.

SEC. 122. Every person elected or appointed to any office, under the provisions of the ninth section of an "Act Incorporating Salt Lake City," approved January 20, 1860, may be removed from such office by **Shall be heard.** a vote of two-thirds of the City Council: *Provided*, that no elective officer shall be removed except for cause; nor unless furnished with the charges against him, and afforded an opportunity of being heard in his defence, and the council shall have power to compel the attendance of witnesses, and the production of papers when necessary, for the purpose of such trial, and shall proceed within ten days to hear and determine the case; and if such officer shall neglect to appear, and answer to such charges, then the council may declare the office vacant. The right of suspension from office, during the pending of such proceedings, shall rest with the Council, and whenever any vacancy shall happen by the death, resignation, or removal of any officer, such vacancy may be filled by the Council.

SEC. 123. If any person elected, or appointed to any office under the corporate authority of this city, **Council to fill vacancies.** shall neglect, or fail to qualify as prescribed by ordinance within thirty days after notification of such election or appointment, the Council may declare such office vacant and proceed to fill the same by appointment.

Sec. 124. Every person elected or appointed to any office shall, before entering upon the duties thereof, take and subscribe an oath or affirmation, that he will support the Constitution of the United States, the laws of this Territory, and the ordinances of this city, and that he will well and truly perform all the duties of his office, to the best of his knowledge and ability; and shall file the same, duly certified by the officer before whom it was taken, in the office of the City Recorder, unless otherwise provided for. *Mode of qualifying*

Sec. 125. All officers appointed by the City Council required by ordinance to give bonds, shall be commissioned by warrant under the corporate seal, signed by the Mayor or presiding officer of the City Council, and Recorder. *Commissioned by warrant.*

Sec. 126. If any person, having been an officer in Salt Lake City shall not, within ten days after notification and request, deliver to his successor in office all property, papers, and effects of every description in his possession belonging to said city, or appertaining to the office he held, he shall be liable to a fine not exceeding one hundred dollars for each day during which he shall so withold said property. *Penalty for failure to deliver effects.*

CHAPTER VII.

CRIMES AND PUNISHMENTS.

Sec. 1. Be it ordained by the City Council of Salt Lake City, that if two or more persons shall engage in a fight within the limits of said City, they shall be liable to a fine in any sum not less than five nor more than one hundred dollars for each offence. *Fighting.* *Penalty.*

Sec. 2. If any person within the limits of said **Assault.** City shall assault another by menacing or threatening, without provocation; or assault and beat another, he **Penalties.** shall be liable to a fine in any sum not exceeding one hundred dollars, or imprisonment not exceeding six months, or to both fine and imprisonment.

Sec. 3. If any person shall abuse or provoke **Insults.** another to an assault, using menacing, insulting, slanderous or profane language in said city, he shall be liable to a fine in any sum not exceeding fifty dollars, **Penalty.** or to imprisonment not exceeding thirty days, or to both fine and imprisonment.

Sec. 4. If any person or persons shall, in a tumultu- **Tumult.** ous manner, commit a disturbance of the peace, within the limits of said city, by brawling or noisy acclamations, by ringing bells, blowing horns or other **Penalty.** noises, they shall be liable to a fine in any sum not exceeding twenty-five dollars.

Sec. 5. When three or more persons assemble **Riots.** together, and in a violent and tumultuous manner, commit an unlawful act; or do a lawful act in an unlawful, violent or tumultuous manner, to the disturbance of the peace, within the limits of said city, it shall be deemed a riot, and every such offender shall be liable to imprisonment not exceeding six months, or to a **Penalties.** fine not exceeding one hundred dollars, or to both fine and imprisonment; and the Mayor or any Alderman is hereby authorized to make proclamation among the persons so assembled, or as near to them as he can **Proclama-** safely come, charging and commanding them, in the **tion.** name of said city to immediately disperse and peacefully to depart to their habitations or lawful pursuits; and if, upon such proclamation being made, such persons shall not obey the same, said Mayor or Alderman may command the Marshal, the Police, and the full power of the city to arrest the offenders, and bring them before him, to be dealt with according to the provisions of this section. *Arrests.*

SEC. 6. Any person neglecting or refusing to give prompt assistance after the making of the aforesaid proclamation, and a call for his services having been made to secure any offenders mentioned in the preceding section shall be liable to imprisonment not exceeding thirty days, or to a fine not exceeding one hundred dollars, or to both fine and imprisonment. *Assistance to be given. Penalties.*

SEC. 7. If any person shall excite disturbance or contention at a public house, court, election, or any meeting of citizens within the limits of said city, he shall be liable to a fine in any sum not exceeding fifty dollars, or to imprisonment not exceeding ten days, or to both fine and imprisonment. *Disturbance. Penalties.*

SEC. 8. Any person who shall disturb a public assembly, congregated for religious or other lawful purposes within the limits of said city, by undue noise, or by unbecoming or indecent behavior, shall be liable to a fine in any sum not exceeding one hundred dollars, or to imprisonment not exceeding six months. *Disturbing public assembly. Penalties.*

SEC. 9. Any person found drunk in any street, lane, alley or other public place in said city, shall be liable to a fine not exceeding twenty-five dollars for each offense, and any person found drunk elsewhere in said city, on complaint being made to any peace officer, shall be liable to arrest and punishment by fine not exceeding twenty dollars. *Drunkenness. Penalty.*

SEC. 10. Any person or persons who shall resist, abuse, or threaten to molest any officer of said city in the exercise of his official duties, or threaten to take or endanger the life of a fellow-being, shall be liable to a fine in any sum not exceeding one hundred dollars, or to imprisonment not more than six months, or to both fine and imprisonment, and may be required to give bonds in any sum not exceeding one thousand dollars, to keep the peace for any term not exceeding six months, and may be imprisoned until such bonds are given, not exceeding a period of six months.

Resisting officer.

Penalties.

SEC. 11. If any person within the limits of this city, convicted of crime and sentenced to imprisonment, shall escape from confinement or custody, he shall be liable to be punished by imprisonment not exceeding the time for which he was first imprisoned, to commence from and after the expiration of the original term of his imprisonment.

Escape of convicts.

Penalty.

SEC. 12. Any person within the limits of this city, who shall aid or assist a person to escape from lawful confinement, or who shall aid or assist another to escape from any peace officer of said city, shall, on conviction, be liable to a fine of not less than five, nor more than one hundred dollars, or to imprisonment not to exceed six months, or to both fine and imprisonment for each offence.

Abetting escape.

Penalty.

SEC. 13. Any person refusing, when called upon by the Marshal or other peace officer of said city, to aid in arresting or securing an offender, shall be liable to a fine in any sum not less than five nor more than fifty dollars for each offence.

Penalty for refusing aid.

SEC. 14. Any person wilfully or maliciously des-

Malicious mischief.

troying or injuring any public or private property, within the limits of said city, shall be liable to a fine in any sum not exceeding one hundred dollars, or to im- *Penalty.* prisonment not exceeding six months, or to both fine and imprisonment.

SEC. 15. If any person shall steal property within *Larceny.* the limits of said city not exceeding twenty dollars in value, he shall be liable to a fine in any sum not exceeding one hundred dollars, or to imprisonment not exceeding six months, or to both fine and imprison- *Penalty.* ment for each offence.

SEC. 16. Any person who shall within the limits *False pretenses.* of this city obtain any goods, chattels or other property under false pretenses, or who shall enter into any public house, shop or place and call for refreshments or other article or thing and receive the same and depart without paying or satisfying the owner thereof, shall be liable to a fine in any sum not exceeding one hundred dollars, or to imprisonment not exceeding six *Penalty.* months, or to both fine and imprisonment.

SEC. 17. Any person who shall wilfully or maliciously kill, maim or disfigure any horse or other *Maiming or poisoning domestic animals.* domestic animal within the limits of said city, the property of another, or maliciously administer poison to any such animals, or expose any poisonous substance, with the intent that the same shall be taken by them, shall be liable to imprisonment for a term not exceeding six months, or to a fine in any sum not exceeding *Penalty.* one hundred dollars, or to both fine and imprisonment.

SEC. 18. Any person who shall torture or cruelly *Cruelty to animals.* beat any horse, ox or other animal, within the limits of said city, whether belonging to himself or any other person, shall be liable to a fine in any sum not exceeding fifty dollars, or imprisonment not exceeding three

Penalties. months, or to both fine and imprisonment.

Fast driving. Sec. 19. Any person who shall, by riding or driving, run any horse, mule or other animal in any of the streets of said city, (unless upon good cause

Penalty. shown,) shall be liable to a fine in any sum not exceeding fifty dollars.

Sec. 20. Any person who shall wilfully or mali-

Destruction of metes and erected, or any tree marked as a boundary of any tract bounds. of land, or city lot, or destroy, deface or alter the marks of any monument, or injure or destroy any shade or fruit tree within the limits of said city, shall be liable to imprisonment, not more than six months, or to a fine

Penalty. of not more than one hundred dollars, or to both fine and imprisonment.

Sec. 21. Any person who shall print, paint, write,

Posting bills without per- tisement, or other device, upon any wall, fence, tree, mission. post, building, or other property, or cause the same to be done without the permission of the owner or agent thereof, within the limits of said city, shall be liable to a fine not exceeding fifty dollars, or to imprisonment

Penalty. not exceeding twenty days, or to both fine and imprisonment for each offence.

Sec. 22. If any person shall, without authority,

Defacing bills. tear down or deface, any ordinance, bill, notice, advertisement or any other paper of a business or legitimate character, lawfully posted up within the limits of said city, within thirty days from the date of such paper, he shall be liable to a fine not exceeding fifty dollars, or to imprisonment not exceeding twenty days, **Penalty.** for every such offence.

SEC. 23. Any person who shall wilfully or maliciously injure, deface or destroy any building or fixture **Malicious destruction of** thereof, or wilfully or maliciously injure, destroy, or **property.** secrete any goods, chattels, or valuable papers of another, or maliciously prepare any deadfall, or dig any pit, or set a gin, or arrange any other trap to injure another's person or property, within the limits of said city, shall be liable to imprisonment for any term not exceeding six months, or to a fine not exceeding one **Penalty.** hundred dollars, or to both fine and imprisonment.

SEC. 24. Any person who shall sell, or expose for sale, any bad beef, pork, mutton, or other meat, stale **Unwholesome food** or otherwise impure flour, meal, grain, or vegetables; or **and drink.** adulterated or unwholesome spirituous or malt liquors, or other beverage intended for drinking, or any other kind of provision, preparation, condiment, or seasoning for meats or drinks, shall be liable to a fine in any sum not exceeding one hundred dollars, or to imprisonment not exceeding six months, or to both fine and imprisonment; and such provision or drinks shall be forfeited to the city, and the court having jurisdiction may order the same to be destroyed. **Penalty.**

SEC. 25. Any person who shall throw, cast, or lay any ashes, offal, vegetables, garbage, dross, cinders, **Deposit of rubbish in** shells, straw, shavings, dirt, filth, or rubbish of any kind **streets prohibited** whatever, in any street, sidewalk, ditch, lane, alley, or public place in this city, except at such place as shall be designated by the Street Supervisor, shall be liable to a fine not exceeding twenty-five dollars for each **Penalty.** offence.

64 CITY ORDINANCES.

Sec. 26. If any person shall keep a house, shop,

Gambling House. or any other place resorted to for the purpose of gambling, or permit or suffer any person in any house, shop or other place under his control or care to play at cards, dice, faro, roulette, keno, or any other game for money or other property, or things representing money, within the limits of said city, such offender for such offence shall be liable to a fine not exceeding one hundred dollars, or to imprisonment not exceeding six

Penalty. months, or to both fine and imprisonment. In a prose-

Keeper. cution under this section, any person who has the charge of, or attends to any such house, shop or place, may be deemed the keeper thereof; and any person

Owner. renting out a house or place for the purpose of gambling, shall be liable to the penalties prescribed in this section.

Sec. 27. Any person who shall play at any game

Gambling of dice, faro, roulette, keno, or other games of chance, resorted to for gambling or fraudulent purposes, for property, money, or things representing money, within the limits of said city, shall be liable to a fine not exceeding one hundred dollars, or to imprisonment not

Penalty. exceeding six months, or to both fine and imprisonment.

Sec. 28. Any person who shall be convicted of

Sabbath breaking. skating, hunting, fishing or any kind of sporting, or who shall keep open any bar, shop, store, or any other place to carry on any kind of business or amusement, or who shall participate in any kind of public amusement, or unnecessary business or labor, or who shall barter, sell, or give away any spirituous, vinous or fermented liquors, except for medicinal or sacramental purposes, within the limits of said city, on the first day of the week, commonly called Sunday, shall be liable to a fine in any sum not exceeding one hundred dollars, or to imprisonment not exceeding three months, or to both fine and imprisonment.

SEC. 29. Any person profaning the name of the Deity within the limits of said city, shall be liable to a fine not exceeding ten dollars, or to imprisonment not exceeding five days, or to both fine and imprisonment. *Profaning*

SEC. 30. Any person who shall sell, circulate or exhibit any obscene print, picture or figure, or any obscene literature, or shall utter or speak any obscene or lewd language, within the limits of said city, shall be liable to a fine not exceeding one hundred dollars, or to imprisonment not exceeding six months, or to both such fine and imprisonment for each offence. *Obscene.*

SEC. 31. Any person who shall be found guilty of designedly making any indecent or obscene exposure of his or her person, or the person of another, or shall indecently exhibit any horse, bull, or other animal; or shall be guilty of lewd or lascivious conduct or prostitution within the limits of said city, shall be deemed guilty of a misdemeanor, and shall be liable to a fine not exceeding one hundred dollars, or to imprisonment not exceeding six months, or to both fine and imprisonment for each offence. *Indecent.*

SEC. 32. If any person shall keep a house of ill-fame, bawdy, or other disorderly house or place resorted to for the purpose of prostitution or lewdness, within the limits of said city, he or she shall be punished by fine not exceeding one hundred dollars, or by imprisonment not exceeding six months, or by both fine and imprisonment. *Prostitution.*

E

SEC. 33. Any person who shall, within the limits of said city, sell or give away, any ardent spirits or other intoxicating liquor to any child under fourteen years of age, or to any apprentice without the consent of his or her master or mistress, or to any Indian, for each offence shall be liable to a fine of not less than five nor more than one hundred dollars, or to imprisonment not exceeding six months, or to both fine and imprison ment.

Liquor.

SEC. 34. Any person who shall use any influence, directly or indirectly, to induce, persuade, or entice any female from her husband, parents, or guardian, or to alienate her feelings therefrom; or who shall use any influence to entice or persuade any minor, male or female, from his or her parents, guardians, or other persons having charge of the same, without the consent of such parents, guardians, or other person, shall be liable to a fine of not more than one hundred dollars, or to imprisonment not more than six months, or to both fine and imprisonment.

Enticing minors.

SEC. 35. Persons within the limits of said city, not having visible means of support, living idly, or who are found loitering about the streets or public places, or lodging in the night time upon the premises of others and not giving an account of themselves, or going about from house to house begging, or placing themselves in the streets or other public places to beg or receive alms, and all keepers or exhibitors of any gaming table or device, and all persons who travel from place to place for the purpose of gambling, and all persons upon whom shall be found any instrument or thing used for the commission of burglary, or for picking

Beggars and gamblers.

locks or pockets, and who cannot give a good account of the possession of the same shall be deemed vagrants.

SEC. 36. It shall be the duty of the Mayor or any Alderman of said city having personal knowledge, or on complaint being made under oath that any person is a vagrant, to cause such person to be brought before him, and if, upon examination, such person be found guilty of vagrancy, he or she shall for each offence be Vagrants. liable to a fine not exceeding fifty dollars, or to imprisonment not exceeding thirty days, or to both fine and imprisonment, and may be required to give bonds with good and sufficient sureties in a penal sum of not less than one hundred nor exceeding one thousand dollars, conditioned that the said defendant will, for the space of six months next ensuing the execution of said bond, be of good behavior, and in default thereof, he or she may be committed to the City prison until such security is given, not exceeding ninety days.

SEC. 37. On the trial of any person charged with being a vagrant, before the Mayor or Alderman, it shall be lawful for the City to introduce, in support of said charge, testimony of the general character and reputation of the defendant, touching the offence or charge set forth in the complaint, and the defendant may also introduce testimony for the purpose of disproving such charge.

SEC. 38. All persons owning swine are hereby forbidden to feed the same upon meat, blood or entrails in a putrid or decayed state, or other unwhole-Feeding swine. some food, calculated to engender disease in the flesh of such animals, under the penalty of not less than five nor more than one hundred dollars; and all fowl, such as turkeys, ducks, geese and hens found running at large at any time between the first day of March and the first day of October, shall be forfeited to and shall be liable to be killed by any person upon whose premises they may be found trespassing.

Fowls at large.

SEC. 39. Any persons discharging guns or pistols within the limits of the city, between the hours of sunset and sun-rise, or on the Sabbath day (except in self-defense, or in the case of any civil officer in the discharge of his duty) shall be liable to a fine of not less than one and more than ten dollars for every such offence.

Discharging guns.

SEC. 40. Any person or persons discharging fire-arms within the limits of the city, without a lawful breastwork or battery, or for the protection of the citizens, shall be liable to a fine of not less than one, nor more than twenty-five dollars for every such offence.

Breast-work.

SEC. 41. A breastwork or battery, for target shooting, to be deemed lawful, shall be a wall eighteen inches thick, six feet wide and six feet high in the back, with side wings one foot thick, each extending two feet, increasing flaringly to the front, and six feet high, of adobies, or mud, or its equivalent of other material.

SEC. 42. The Mayor is authorized and empowered to grant full pardons for violations of the ordinances of said city, or to remit so much of any fine or penalty as belongs to the city, together with costs of prosecution, when to him it shall seem just and reasonable.

Pardons.

Sec. 43. It shall be the duty of the Mayor to report quarterly to the City Council the number of fines *Reports.* remitted and pardons granted.

———o———

CHAPTER VIII.

RELATING TO LICENSES.

———

ARTICLE I.

MANNER OF OBTAINING, ISSUING AND RECORDING LICENSES.

Sec. 1. Be it ordained, by the City Council of Salt Lake City, that it shall not be lawful for any person or persons to engage in any business hereinafter mentioned, without first obtaining a license therefor.

Sec. 2. All applications for License shall be made in writing to the Mayor, and the amount, as hereinafter provided, shall be paid in advance to the City Treasurer. All Licenses shall be issued and signed by the Mayor, or presiding officer of the City Council, and attested by the City Recorder under the Seal of the City. The Recorder shall keep an alphabetical list of Licenses issued, stating the number, name, time, place and kind of business, and the amount paid, with such remarks as may be considered necessary. *How to obtain license.*

ARTICLE II.

BANKS, BANKERS, BROKERS, AND EXCHANGE DEALERS.

Checks etc.

SEC. 1. No person, corporation, association or company, shall carry on the business of dealing in, buying or selling, or discounting any kind of bills of exchange, checks, drafts, bank notes, promissory notes, bonds or other kinds of writings obligatory; or in gold, silver, or bullion, within this City, without first obtaining a License under the provisions of this article.

Amount of Capital.

SEC. 2. Each bank, banker, broker, or exchange dealer, on making application for License, shall make a statement under oath, sworn to before the Mayor or City Recorder, of the amount of capital to be employed; such statements shall be filed in alphabetical order, and yearly licenses may be issued thereon, as follows, viz:

With Capital of $300,000 and over, $500 per annum.

With Capital of $200,000, and less than $300,000, $300 per annum.

With Capital of $100,000, and less than $200,000, $200 per annum.

With Capital of less than $100,000, and over $50,000, $100 per annum.

With Capital of $50,000 or less, $50 per annum.

ARTICLE III.

MERCHANTS.

SEC. 1.   Whosoever shall deal in buying or selling goods, wares or merchandise at any store, stand or place within this city is declared to be a merchant.

SEC. 2.   Each merchant, on making application to the Mayor for license, shall make a statement of the cash value of all goods, wares and other merchandise which he may have in his possession or under his control, whether owned by him or consigned to him for sale, which statement shall be sworn to, before the Mayor or the City Recorder, by the merchant making it, or his duly authorized agent: *Provided* that if any merchant shall increase his stock beyond the limit of his class of business during the period of his license, he shall procure an additional license for such increase.

value of goods.

SEC. 3.   The Recorder shall file all such statements in alphabetical order, and yearly licenses may be issued thereon, as follows, viz. :—

Over $500,000 shall constitute 1st class, and pay $500.00.

Over $400,000 and not exceeding $500,000 shall constitute 2nd class, and pay $450.00

Over $300,000 and not exceeding $400,000 shall constitute 3rd class, and pay $400.00

Over $200,000 and not exceeding $300,000 shall constitute 4th class, and pay $350.00.

Over $100,000 and not exceeding $200,000 shall constitute 5th class, and pay $300.00

Over $75,000 and not exceeding $100,000 shall constitute 6th class, and pay $250.00.

Over $60,000 and not exceeding $75,000 shall constitute 7th class, and pay $225.00.

Over $50,000 and not exceeding $60,000 shall constitute 8th class, and pay $200.00.

Over $40,000 and not exceeding $50,000 shall constitute 9th class, and pay $175.00.

Over $30,000 and not exceeding $40,000 shall constitute 10th class, and pay $150.00.

Over $20,000 and not exceeding $30,000 shall constitute 11th class, and pay $125.00.

Over $15,000 and not exceeding $20,000 shall constitute 12th class, and pay $100.00.

Over $10,000 and not exceeding $15,000 shall constitute 13th class, and pay $90.00.

Over $8,000 and not exceeding $10,000 shall constitute 14th class and pay $80.00.

Over $5,000 and not exceeding $8,000 shall constitute 15th class, and pay $70.00.

Over $4,000 and not exceeding $5,000 shall constitute 16th class, and pay $60.00.

Over $3,000 and not exceeding $4,000 shall constitute 17th class, and pay $50.00.

Over $2,000 and not exceeding $3,000 shall constitute 18th class, and pay $40.00

Over $1,000 and not exceeding $2,000 shall constitute 19th class, and pay $30.00.

Not exceeding $1,000 shall constitute 20th class, and pay $25.00.

SEC. 4.   The provisions of this Article shall not be construed to authorize any person to sell spirituous, vinous or fermented liquors in any quantity.

ARTICLE IV.

HOTEL-KEEPERS.

SEC. 1. Whoever shall keep any public house with lodging rooms for the accommodation of guests within this city, is declared to be a tavern or hotel keeper.

SEC. 2. Each tavern or hotel keeper, on making application to the Mayor for license, shall make a statement of the number of rooms of all kinds his house contains, which statement shall be sworn to before the Mayor or the City Recorder, by the tavern or hotel keeper, or his duly authorized agent.

Number of rooms.

SEC. 3. The Recorder shall file all such statements in alphabetical order, and yearly licenses may-be issued thereon, as follows, viz:

Over 100 rooms shall constitute 1st class, and shall pay $200.00.

Over 75 to 100 rooms shall constitute 2nd class, and shall pay $150.00.

Over 50 to 75 rooms shall constitute 3rd class, and shall pay $100.00

Over 25 to 50 rooms shall constitute 4th class, and shall pay $50.00.

25 rooms and under shall constitute 5th class, and shall pay $25.00.

Provided, licenses be gran'ed f·· lodging rooms exclusively at half the foregoing rates.

ARTICLE V.

RESTAURANTS.

SEC. 1. Whoever shall keep any house cr place for furnishing meals without lodging within this city is declared to be a restaurant keeper.

SEC. 2. Each restaurant keeper, on making application to the Mayor for license, shall make a statement of the greatest number of persons he can furnish with meals at one time, which statement shall be sworn to, before the Mayor or City Recorder, by the restaurant keeper or his duly authorized agent.

Number of meals.

SEC. 3. The City Recorder shall file all such statements, and yearly licenses may be issued thereon as follows, viz:

For all restaurants able to accommodate thirty or more guests at one time, $75.00.

For all restaurants unable to accommodate thirty guests at one time, $40.00.

SEC. 4. A license may be issued to hotel and resaturant keepers to sell spirituous and fermented liquors at their places of business, in bottles to their guests at meals only, on payment into the City Treasury of the sum of two hundred dollars per annum, subject to the proviso in said Ordinance.

Bottled liquors at meals.

ARTICLE VI.

LIVERY AND FEED STABLE KEEPERS.

SEC. 1. A livery stable keeper is one who keeps for hire—horses, carriages or other vehicles, and a feed stable keeper is one who provides feed and stabling for animals not his own.

SEC. 2. Each livery stable keeper, on making application to the Mayor for license, shall make a statement of the greatest number of animals and vehicles of all descriptions to be kept by him, which statement shall be sworn to, before the Mayor or City Recorder, by the livery stable keeper or his duly authorized agent.

Number of animals and vehicles.

SEC. 3. The City Recorder shall file all such statements, and may issue yearly licenses thereon as follows, viz:

For 10 vehicles and over, with animals, $100.00 per annum.

For 5 to 10 vehicles, with animals, $60.00 per annum.

For less than 5 vehicles, with animals, $30.00 per annum.

For feeding stables exclusively, $25.00.

ARTICLE VII.

BILLIARDS AND PIN ALLEYS.

SEC. 1. A keeper of a billiard table is one who possesses or keeps, or has the control or management of, one or more billiard tables whereon others are permitted to play, and for the use of which, or privilege of playing thereon, or for the hire thereof, any money or its equivalent, or any check or counter in lieu of money, shall be paid or received; and all billiard tables within the city shall be held and taken to be so kept, and to come within the meaning and provisions of this Article, except such as may be kept within dwelling houses for owners' recreation, and not for the purpose of letting the same to others to play thereon for money, or anything representing, or in lieu of money, or for wagers or bets; and there shall be levied and collected for every license to keep billiard tables as aforesaid—

For one table for three months, $100.00.
" two tables " " $175.00.
" three tables " " $225.00.

And each additional table for three months, $25.00. And each table shall be numbered, and license therefor taken and paid for, for three months in advance.

SEC. 2. That there shall be levied and collected for every license to keep bagatelle, borondelette, pigeon-hole, or other kinds of tables, on which games are played, other than billiard tables, for each table the sum of twenty-five dollars per quarter, payable quarterly in advance. And no such table or billiard tables shall be kept in any saloon, or any other public place for use, without a license therefor shall be first obtained, according to the provisions of this Ordinance.

SEC. 3. A keeper of a pin alley is one who owns, possesses, or keeps such alley, (without regard to the number of pins used,) on which persons are permitted to play; and for license to keep a pin alley there shall be levied and collected quarterly, in advance, the sum of $25.00 on each alley or runway. *Pin alleys.*

SEC. 4. All persons obtaining license under this Article shall give bonds to the City of Salt Lake, with at least two sureties, to be approved by the Mayor, in the penal sum of $500.00, conditioned that the party so licensed shall faithfully observe and keep all the provisions of this Article, and that he will prohibit music, dancing, drunkenness and all riotous or disorderly conduct on his premises. *Bonds.*

ARTICLE VIII.

Sundry Avocations.

SEC. 1. It shall not be lawful for any person to exercise within this city, the business of runner or buyer on the street, real estate or land agent, smelting and crushing ores, assaying, bill poster, conveyancer, dentist, physician, surgeon, oculist, aurist, insurance agents, photographers, machine agents, expressing, telegraphing, intelligence office, running omnibuses, cars, cabs, drays or other vehicle, carting, porterage, packing, bootblacks, or of peddling of fruit, or to conduct or manage any theatre, circus, menagerie, exhibition, show or amusement, skating rink, shooting gallery, ball or concert, without first obtaining a license therefor.

SEC. 2. Whoever exercises the calling or profession of any business described in the preceding section shall be considered to come within the meaning of this Article.

SEC. 3. There shall be levied and collected yearly, in advance, unless otherwise provided, for every license granted for the business or object herein specified, as follows:

First. Upon a runner's license $25.00.

Second. Upon a real estate or land agent's license $25.00.

Third. Upon a license for smelting or crushing ore $100.00.

Fourth. Upon an assayer's license $25.00.

Fifth. Upon a bill poster's license $10.00.

Sixth. Upon a conveyancer's license $25.00.

Seventh. Upon a dentist's license $25.00.

Eighth. Upon a physician's license $25.00.

Ninth. Upon a surgeon's license $25.00.

Tenth. Upon an oculist's license $25.00.

Eleventh. Upon an aurist's license $25.00.

Twelfth. Upon an insurance agent's license, for each company represented, $25.00.

Thirteenth. Upon a photographer's license $25.00.

Fourteenth. Upon a machine agent's license, for each company represented, $50.00.

Fifteenth. Upon a boot black's license $2.00.

Sixteenth. Upon a license for a theatre $200.00

Seventeenth. Upon a license for a skating rink $100.00.

Eighteenth. Upon a license for a shooting gallery $50.00.

Nineteenth. Upon a license for a concert, ball, lecture, tricks of legerdemain, or any other exhibition, show or amusement, $5.00 for each performance or exhibition.

Twentieth. Upon a license for a circus or equestrian exhibition $50.00 for each performance or exhibition.

Twenty-first. Upon a license for a travelling menagerie $25.00 for each performance or exhibition.

Twenty-second, Upon a license to run an omnibus or car $25.00.

Twenty-third. Upon a license to run a hack or cab $20.00.

Twenty-fourth. Upon a license to run a dray or job wagon $10.00.

Twenty-fifth. Upon a license for telegraphing $25.00.

Twenty-sixth. Upon a porter's license $10.00.

Twenty-seventh. Upon an express agent's or company's license $100.00.

Twenty-eighth. Upon an intelligence office keeper's license $25.00.

Twenty-ninth. Upon a fruit peddler's license $5.00.

ARTICLE IX.

SUNDRY PROVISIONS.

SEC. 1. Licenses may be issued for all purposes or branches of business named in this Ordinance for terms of three months, on payment of 15 per cent additional, Term of licenses.

and for terms of six months on payment of 10 per cent additional.

SEC. 2. Sellers of fresh meat, poultry and fish are required to be located and do business within the city market, or on market grounds, and when so located their license shall be considered to be included in the rent of their stalls or stands.

Meat, poultry, fish.

SEC. 3. Licenses shall not be valid if the business is transferred from the building where it was originally granted, unless such transfer be recorded in the City Recorder's office.

Transfer.

SEC. 4. It shall not be lawful for any person within this city to engage in the business of peddling or hawking merchandise, or to conduct, manage, or sell tickets for a lottery or gift enterprise, or any kind of fraudulent device or practice, for the purpose of selling or disposing of merchandise or goods of any description, with or without tickets, numbered or marked for that purpose.

Peddling.

SEC. 5. All licenses for billiard tables, pin and bowling alleys, tavern keepers, keepers of ordinaries, victualling or coffee-houses, restaurants, exhibitions of showmen, shows of every kind, concerts or musical entertainments, circuses, theatrical performances, exhibitions or amusements may be withheld at the discretion of the Mayor; *Provided*, an appeal may be taken to the City Council, whose decision thereon shall be final.

May be withheld.

The City Council may, by resolution at any time, limit the number of licenses to be issued for any kind of business provided for in this Ordinance.

Limit.

SEC. 6. Whoever shall violate any of the provisions of the several articles of this Ordinance, or refuse to comply with any of the requirements thereof, shall be deemed guilty of a misdemeanor, and, on conviction thereof, shall be liable to a fine in any sum not exceeding one hundred dollars, or to imprisonment not exceeding six months, or both fine and imprisonment. *Provided:* That the penalty shall in no case exceed twice the amount of the yearly license of the party accused for each offense. Violate.

SEC. 7. That all ordinances or parts of ordinances conflicting with the foregoing, be, and the same are, hereby repealed. Repealed.

———o———

CHAPTER IX.

LICENSING AND REGULATING THE MANUFACTURE AND SALE OF SPIRITUOUS AND FERMENTED LIQUORS.

SEC. 1. Be it ordained by the City Council of Salt Lake City, that no person shall, within the corporate limits of said city, directly or indirectly, in person or by another, manufacture, sell, barter, or otherwise dispose of, or permit to be manufactured, bartered or delivered, for or on his account, any spirituous or fermented liquors without a license first obtained according to the provisions of this ordinance, as a dram Dispose of.

F

or tippling shop-keeper, liquor dealer, wine dealer, beer saloon keeper, distiller or brewer.

SEC. 2. A dram or tippling shop-keeper is a person who sells spirituous and fermented liquors to be drunk at the place of sale. A liquor dealer is a person who sells spirituous and fermented liquors not to be drunk at the place of sale. A wine dealer is a person who sells wine exclusively. A beer saloon-keeper is a person who sells beer, ale or porter. A distiller is a person who manufactures spirituous liquors, *Provided:* That the same shall not be sold to be drunk on the premises without first obtaining a license as a dram or tippling shop-keeper. A brewer is a person who manufactures fermented liquors.

Classes of dealers.

SEC. 3. Applications for License under this Ordinance shall be made in writing to the Mayor, and shall state where the business is to be carried on, the kind of business, the full name of the applicant, and if a firm the full name of each member thereof.

Application.

SEC. 4. On payment to the City Treasurer of the amount herein named, and on the fulfillment of all other requirements of this Ordinance, the Mayor may issue Licenses to applicants to carry on the business asked for, for the period of three months, in the tenement designated in the application, at the following rates, viz:

Licenses

As a dram and tippling shop-keeper, two hundred and fifty dollars.

As a liquor dealer, one hundred and fifty dollars.

As a wine dealer, seventy-five dollars.

As a beer-saloon keeper, one hundred dollars.

As a distiller, one hundred and fifty dollars.

As a brewer one hundred dollars.

And the number of Licenses may at any time be limited by the Council, under this ordinance. _{Limit.}

SEC. 5. No License granted under this ordinance shall be assignable or transferable, or authorize any person or persons other than those named in the License to carry on the business therein specified; and no person or persons shall carry on any business provided for in this Ordinance at any other place than the one designated in such License ; *Provided:* That the City Council may, on application by the parties interested, authorize the assignment of the License, or a change in the place of business. _{Not transferable.}

SEC. 6. The Mayor, whenever in his judgment the peace, good order or safety of the City or its inhabitants shall require it, and on Municipal, County or Territorial election days, Fourth of July, Decoration, Thanksgiving and all Territorial and National holidays, may, by proclamation, forbid the sale, giving away, or in any way disposing of spirituous or fermented liquors for any given period, not to exceed twenty-four hours at any one time ; and any person who shall sell, barter or give away, any spirituous or fermented liquors in contravention of said proclamation shall, on conviction, be fined in the sum of fifty dollars for each offense, any license to the contrary notwithstanding. _{No sale on holidays.}

SEC. 7. Any person obtaining License under this Ordinance shall be subject to the following regulations: He shall faithfully observe and keep all ordinances in force in relation to liquor during the period of such license; he shall not keep open his bar, house or place for the sale of liquors, nor sell, give away, nor in any manner deal in by himself, servant, or other person, _{Closing.}

any spirituous or fermented liquors between the hours
of ten o'clock p. m. and six o'clock a. m., on any day
of the week; he shall prohibit all gaming, with or without betting, by means of dominoes, cards, dice, or other
articles, every game of chance, and every other description of gaming or gambling; and, on the proclamation of the Mayor for all liquor establishments to be
closed, he shall discontinue business during the period
of such proclamation. He shall not in any wise dispose
of liquors to any person under fourteen years of age,
nor to any Indian; he shall prohibit music, dancing,
drunkenness and all riotous or disorderly conduct on
his premises.

No gaming, etc.

SEC. 8. If any person shall keep any house or
place within the corporate limits of this city, for the
purpose of manufacturing, selling, or otherwise disposing of spirituous or fermented liquors, or shall manufacture, sell, or otherwise dispose of spirituous or
fermented liquors as provided in this Ordinance, without first having obtained a license therefor, as herein
provided, on conviction thereof he shall forfeit and
pay a fine of one hundred dollars for the first offense,
and if convicted of a second offense a fine of one hundred dollars and imprisonment for thirty days; and for
a third or subsequent conviction a fine of one hundred
dollars and imprisonment for the term of six months.

Fines.

SEC. 9. Any person violating any of the provisions of this Ordinance, for which no penalty is herein
otherwise provided, shall forfeit and pay a fine of fifty
dollars for each offense.

SEC. 10. All ordinances and parts of ordinances
relating to the manufacture or sale of spirituous or fermented liquors, in conflict herewith, are hereby repealed;

Repealed.

Provided the repeal of such ordinances shall not affect any rights accrued or liabilities for fines and penalties incurred; but all such rights and liabilities may be maintained and enforced the same as if said ordinances and parts of ordinances had remained in full force.

———o ———

CHAPTER X.

AUTHORIZING THE MAYOR TO GRANT PERMITS TO SELL LIQUORS AND WINES.

Be it resolved by the City Council of Salt Lake City, that the Mayor of said City be and is hereby authorized to grant Permits, signed by the Recorder, and sealed with the Corporate Seal, to any person or persons, to sell or dispose of any stated quantity, by wholesale in any one Permit, not exceeding five barrels of Wine, Spirituous or Fermented Liquors; *Provided:* That a reasonable sum therefor, to be determined by the Mayor, shall be paid into the City Treasury.

CHAPTER XI.

IN RELATION TO ISSUING LICENSES FOR LIQUOR, BAR AND
BEER ESTABLISHMENTS; ALSO FOR BILLIARD
SALOONS AND BOWLING ALLEYS.

————

Be it resolved by the City Council of Salt Lake City,
that no Liquor, Bar, Beer, Billiard Saloon, or Bowling
Alley Licenses shall hereafter be granted by said
Council for a shorter term than three months, and in
all cases such licenses shall be paid quarterly in advance.

————0————

CHAPTER XII.

RELATING TO RAILROADS.

————

SEC. 1. Be it ordained by the City Council of Salt
Lake City, that all companies constructing Railroads
within the limits of said City shall be subject to the
following regulations: The grantees of all Railroads,
shall, at their own expense, construct and keep in good
repair all water sects, sewers, drains, street crossings,
or receiving basins, and all fixtures connected therewith, and the distribution of water in said City as

Regula-
tions.

may be affected thereby. The construction, alterations and repairs to be done under the direction of the City Water Master, subject to the approval of the City Council.

SEC. 2. That it shall especially be incumbent on all railroad companies, at their own expense, to construct arches and bridges for all the cross streets, now or hereafter to be made, which will be intersected by Bridges, etc. the embankments, or excavations of their railroads, and also to make such embankments or excavations, as in the opinion of the City Council, may be required to make the passage over the railroad and embankments easy and convenient for all the purposes for which streets are usually used; and also all such drains and sewers, as their embankments and excavations may make necessary. And, further, that the said companies shall make their railroad paths conform to what is or may hereafter be the regulation or grade of the street Grade. or place through which their railroads pass; and no company shall have the right to take up, remove, carry away, or cause, or permit to be taken up, removed or carried away, any rock, gravel, earth or other material from any street or public place, for making embankments, grades, or for any other purpose, except by permission of the City Council, and under the direction of the street supervisor.

SEC. 3. That if, at any time after the construction of any railroad, it shall appear to the City Council that any part thereof shall constitute an obstruction or impediment to the ordinary use of any street or place, or be Obstructions. run contrary to the regulations of the City, the said railroad company or the officers thereof, shall, on the requisition of the City Council, forthwith provide a remedy for the same, satisfactory to said Council; or, if they fail to find such remedy, they shall, within one month after such requisition, proceed to remove such railroad obstruction or impediment, and to replace the street or place in as good condition as it was before the said railroad was laid down; and should the said company or officers neglect or refuse to obey such requisition, the City Council may, upon the expiration of the time limited in such notice, cause the obstruction or impediment to be removed, and the street or place restored, as aforesaid, at the expense of the said railroad company.

Sec. 4. That nothing in any ordinance or resolution granting right of way, or franchise for railroad, shall be construed to prohibit any other railroad company **Crossing tracks** from crossing any railroad track already laid, and when any railroad shall intersect any other railroad, the rails of each shall be so cut or altered as to permit the cars to pass without obstruction; and any person wilfully obstructing any railroad herein provided for, shall, on conviction thereof, be liable to a fine in any sum not exceeding one hundred dollars, or imprisonment not exceeding six months, or to both fine and imprisonment.

Sec. 5. That the tracks of all railroads shall be laid in the centre of the streets, unless otherwise directed by the City Council, and all trains running therein are **Speed.** hereby prohibited from running at a greater speed than eight miles per hour; and the bells on locomotives in motion shall in all cases be rung continuously in the inhabited portions of the City, and all trains are required to come to a full stop before crossing any other line of railroad, and at a distance of not less than ten feet therefrom ; and when two trains arrive at the same crossing simultaneously, the train on the first construct-ed track shall have precedence in crossing, and no train, engine, or cars shall be allowed to stand in the street, or upon the sidewalks or crossing to obstruct the ordinary travel thereon. Any violation of the provisions of this section, shall render the offender liable to a fine in any sum not exceeding one hundred dollars, or imprisonment not exceeding six months, or to both fine and imprisonment.

SEC. 6. That the right of regulating the description of power to be used in the City in propelling cars on and along railroads, and the speed of the same, togeth-er with the price of the license or tax to be paid there-for, shall not, by virtue of any grant, or contract, be construed to mean that such right passes to the grantee ; but such rights, together with all other powers vested in said Council for the regulating, controling or removing of railroads within said City, be and the same are expressly retained and reserved.

Rights reserved.

———o——. -

CHAPTER XIII.

SALT LAKE CITY RAILROAD COMPANY.

ARTICLE I.

SEC. 1. *Be it resolved* by the City Council of Salt Lake City, that the "Salt Lake City Railroad Company," its successors and assigns, have the authority and consent of the City Council, and the permission is hereby granted it, to construct and operate a single or double track Street Railroad, together with all the necessary switches, for the accommodation of said road, on the following streets of said City, commencing at the intersection of Third West and South Temple Streets,

Location of road. thence east on South Temple Street to West Temple Street, thence south on said street to First South Street, thence east on said street to East Temple Street, thence south on said street to Third South Street, thence east on said street to First East Street, thence north on said street to First South Street, thence west on said street to East Temple Street, thence north on said street to South Temple Street, thence west on said street to West Temple Street, and from the intersection of First South and First East Streets, east on First South Street to or near the eastern limit of said City; and from the intersection of South Temple and Second West Streets, north on Second West Street to the Warm Springs; also from the intersection of Third West and South Temple Streets to North Temple Street, thence West on North Temple Street, to or near the Jordan Bridge, on the following conditions, *viz*: Such track or tracks to be laid on such grades as are now, or may hereafter be, established by the City Council. In consideration of this franchise, the grantee, its successors and assigns

Repairs. aforesaid are hereby required to keep in good repair the space inside the track, and a space one foot each side of the same, and also to use no steam power on any part of the road for propelling cars, unless permitted by the City Council. And the grantees aforesaid shall place cars on said railroad, with all necessary modern improvements for the convenience and comfort of passengers, which shall be run thereon, each and every day, both ways, as often as the public convenience _{Speed.} may require, and at a rate of speed not exceeding eight miles per hour, and under such regulations as the City Council may from time to time prescribe, *Provided:* That the grantees aforesaid shall comply with the directions of the City Council in the construction of said Railroad, and in any other matter connected with the regulations of the same, and that the track or tracks shall be constructed in the centre of the streets, unless otherwise directed by the City Council, and in such manner as shall be approved by the Street Supervisor, _{Water-courses.} so as to cause no unnecessary impediment to the common and ordinary use of said streets for all other purposes; and that the water courses of said streets be left free and unobstructed; said track to be laid upon a good foundation, with a tram rail, unless otherwise authorized by the City Council, even with the surface of the roadway; and good and permanent crossings shall be made by the grantees aforesaid at the intersection of streets and elsewhere whenever the same shall be necessary, under the direction of the Street Supervisor. And said track shall not be suffered to be unnecessarily obstructed by wagons, carriages or other _{Price of passage.} vehicles or any other thing whatsoever. The price of a single passage shall not exceed fifteen cents, and the grantees aforesaid shall conspicuously post in each car a schedule of fares, which shall have previously been approved by the City Council, and no charge shall be made in excess thereof; and from and after the year one thousand eight hundred and seventy-seven (1877), the grantee, its successors and assigns may be subject to a *per capita* tax, not exceeding five mills ($\frac{1}{2}$ cent) _{Tax.} for each passenger carried. Said road shall be commenced within six months, and a single track completed and the cars running thereon, from the said intersection

of Third West and South Temple Streets, thence east
on South Temple Street to West Temple Street, thence
south on said street to First South Street, thence east on
said street to East Temple Street, thence south on said
street to Third South Street, thence east on said street
to First East Street, thence north on said street to First
South Street, thence east on said street to Second East
Street, within twelve months after the passage of this
Resolution, April 26, 1872. The said road shall be
free from City tax until the year one thousand, eight
hundred and seventy four (1874).

SEC. 2.   *And be it further resolved*, that this franchise is granted for the term of twenty-one years from
and after the date of the passage of this Resolution,
Term of   April 26, 1872, and accepted on the following conditions,
franchise. *viz* : That if the grantee, its successors or assigns shall
fail to keep and perform all the stipulations of this
Resolution, the City Council after sixty days notice, and
on failure on the part of said company to provide a
remedy or make satisfactory arrangements therefor,
may, by a two thirds vote, declare the privileges herein
granted forfeited, and proceed to take possession of
the road bed, and control the same as if this Resolution had not been passed.

SEC. 3.   *And be it further resolved*, that if said
grantees shall refuse or neglect to comply with the
rules, regulations and ordinances of said City Council
Fine.   relating to Railroads and running of cars within the
corporate limits of said City, they shall be liable to a
fine in any sum not exceeding one hundred dollars for
each offence.

SEC. 4.   *And be it further resolved*, that if this

grant, with the terms and conditions herein contained, be not accepted in writing by said grantee within sixty (60) days after the passage of this Resolution, April 26, 1872, the same shall become void and of none effect.

ARTICLE II.

Granting to the Salt Lake City Railroad Company, the right to construct and operate a Street Railroad on certain streets in said City.

SEC. 1. *Be it resolved* by the City Council of Salt Lake City, that the right to construct and operate a Street Railroad, from the intersection of South Temple and First West Streets, north on said First West Street Location. to the intersection thereof with Third North Street and from thence west on said Third North Street to the intersection thereof with Second West Street, be, and the same is, hereby granted to the said Salt Lake City Railroad Company, for the term of twenty-one (21) years, dated from the 26th day of April, A. D. eighteen hundred and seventy-two (1872), and subject to the same conditions, obligations, restrictions and provisions as are contained in a Resolution of said City Council granting to said Railroad Company the right to construct and operate a Street Railroad on certain streets therein named, approved April 26th A. D. eighteen hundred and seventy-two (1872).

ARTICLE III.

Granting to the Salt Lake City Railroad Company the right to construct and operate a Street Railroad on Third South Street in said City.

Be it resolved by the City Council of Salt Lake City,

that the right to construct and operate a Street Railroad from the intersection of First East Street and Third South Street, thence east to the intersection of Fourth East Street and Third South Street, be, and the same is, hereby granted to the Salt Lake City Railroad Company, for the term of twenty-one (21) years, dating from the twenty-sixth day of April, 1872 ; and subject to the same conditions, obligations, restrictions and provisions as are contained in a Resolution of said Council, granting to said Railroad Company the right to construct and operate a Street Railroad on certain streets therein named, approved April 26th, 1872.

ARTICLE IV.

Granting to the Salt Lake City Railroad Company the right to use the T Rail, and extending the time for the completion of certain portions of said Company's Line of Railroad.

SEC. 1. *Be it resolved* by the City Council of Salt Lake City: That the Salt Lake City Railroad Company have and are hereby granted the right to use the T Rail on any of the streets of said City on which their track may hereafter be laid during the pleasure of the Council.

Term ex-
tended.

SEC. 2. That the time specified in the Charter of the Salt Lake City Railroad Company, approved April 26th, 1872, for the completion of said Company's line of Railroad on First East Street, from Third South Street to First South Street, be and the same is hereby extended, during the pleasure of said Company, to any period within the limits of their charter.

Sec. 3. That the time specified in said Charter for the completion of said Company's line of Railroad on First South Street, from First East Street to Second East Street, be, and the same is, hereby extended for the term of six months.

Sec. 4. This Resolution to be in force from and after its passage.

A R T I C L E V.

Granting to the Salt Lake City Railroad Company the right to construct and operate a Street Railroad on certain streets in said City.

Be it resolved by the City Council of Salt Lake City, that the right to construct and operate a double track railway from south and east of the Temple Block, east on South Temple Street five blocks to Fir or Oak Street, thence north on one of said streets three blocks to Bluff Street, thence east on Bluff Street to or near the eastern limits of the City, with the privilege of laying a T rail, be and the same is hereby granted to the Salt Lake City Railroad Company, subject to the same conditions, obligations, restrictions and provisions as are contained in a resolution of said Council, granting to said Street Railroad Company the right to construct and operate a street railroad on certain streets therein named, approved April 26th, 1872, and for the same term, dating from the 26th day of April, 1872.

Location.

CHAPTER XIV.

ARTICLE I.

RELATING TO THE MANUFACTURE AND DISTRIBUTION
OF GAS.

SEC. 1. Be it ordained by the City Council of
Salt Lake City, that P. Lalor Sherry, George A.
Smith, James Jack, Thomas Williams and Thomas W.
Ellerbeck, their associates, heirs, successors and assigns, are hereby vested with the right to manufacture
gas and the privilege of using the streets, lanes and
alleys of said City, for the purpose of conveying the
same in said City, and to the citizens thereof for the
term of twenty-one years from and after the date of the
passage of this ordinance.

Term of
franchise.

SEC. 2. That the said P. Lalor Sherry, George
A. Smith, James Jack, Thomas Williams and Thomas
W. Ellerbeck, their associates, heirs, successors and
assigns, shall have and are hereby granted the right
and authority to use the streets, lanes and alleys of
said City for the introduction of pipes and other
apparatus for gas; *Provided:* That such streets, lanes
and alleys, shall be repaired to the satisfaction of the said
City Council within a reasonable time ; *and provided
also*, that the said streets, lanes and alleys shall not at
any time be unnecessarily obstructed, and all gas pipes
shall be laid under the direction of the City Council
of said City.

Use of
streets.

SEC. 3. That in consideration of the privileges hereby granted to the said P. Lalor Sherry, George A. Smith, James Jack, Thomas Williams and Thomas W. Ellerbeck, their associates, heirs, successors and assigns, they, the said P. Lalor Sherry, George A. Smith, James Jack, Thomas Williams, and Thomas W. Ellerbeck, their associates, heirs, successors and assigns shall construct their works and furnish gas for the said City and citizens thereof within one year from the date of the passage of this ordinance: *Provided*, That the price of gas so furnished to the citizens of said City shall not, during the existence of this franchise, exceed four dollars per one thousand cubic feet, nor shall the price of gas so furnished for the use of said City exceed the lowest average price at which gas shall or may be furnished to the private citizens as aforesaid ; *and, provided further*, that the quality of gas so furnished shall be as good as is or may be furnished to any other city in any of the Territories of the United States, or in the Pacific States; and such gas to be furnished as aforesaid shall be subjected from time to time, as said City Council may direct, to such test as shall determine its quality; and such gas shall be furnished as aforesaid in such quantity as the said City Council may at any time require for public lamps and for public use.

Price of gas.

Quality subject to test.

SEC. 4. That it shall be the duty of said P. Lalor Sherry, George A. Smith, James Jack, Thomas Williams and Thomas W. Ellerbeck, their associates, heirs, successors and assigns, to lay gas mains and pipes in the said streets, lanes and alleys to the extent and within such times as shall be stipulated in such articles of agreement as may or shall be entered into by and between said City Council and the said P.

Laying pipes.

G

Lalor Sherry, George A. Smith, James Jack, Thomas Williams and Thomas W. Ellerbeck, their associates, heirs, successors and assigns, in pursuance of and not inconsistent with the provisions of this ordinance.

SEC. 5. That the Mayor of said City is hereby Mayor to authorized to sign all such contracts or articles of sign con- agreement as hereinbefore provided, and affix thereto tracts. the corporate seal of said City. All such contracts or articles of agreement to be executed in duplicate, one of which shall be delivered to said P. Lalor Sherry, George A. Smith, James Jack, Thomas Williams and Thomas W. Fllerbeck, their associates, heirs, successors and assigns, the other to be filed in the office of the City Recorder of said City.

SEC. 6. That the said P. Lalor Sherry, George A. Smith, James Jack, Thomas Williams, and Thomas W. Ellerbeck, their associates, heirs, successors and Location of gas assigns, shall submit their proposed location for gas works. works to, and obtain the approval thereof by, the City Council of said City.

SEC. 7. That the privileges hereby granted shall not be forfeited by any temporary failure on the part Tempora- ry failure. of the said P. Lalor Sherry, George A. Smith, James Jack, Thomas Williams and Thomas W. Ellerbeck, their associates, heirs, successors and assigns, to comply with and perform any of the conditions from them exacted in this ordinance, or any contract or articles of agreement made in pursuance hereof as hereinbefore provided : *Provided*, such failures be remedied within a reasonable time.

ARTICLE II.

Articles of agreement made in duplicate, and entered into by and between *Salt Lake City*, a municipal corporation, by the Mayor of said city, party of the first part, and *P. Lalor Sherry, George A. Smith, Thomas W. Ellerbeck, James Jack* and *Thomas Williams*, who, by virtue of an ordinance passed by the City Council of Salt Lake City, March 8th, 1872, entitled "An Ordinance relating to the Manufacture and Distribution of Gas," have been vested with the right and privilege of using the streets, lanes and alleys of said City for the purpose of conveying gas to the said City and citizens thereof, for the term of twenty-one years from the date of the passage of said ordinance party of the second part *Witnesseth* that the said party of the first part, for, and in consideration of, the promises, covenants, and agreements of the said party of the second part, hereinafter set forth, *doth hereby* covenant and agree to and with the said party of the second part, their heirs, successors and assigns, as follows, viz. : That from the present time and until the complete expiration of a term of ten years from the eighth day of March, A. D., eighteen hundred and seventy-two (1872), the said party of the second part, their heirs, successors and assigns, shall have, and hereby are granted, the sole right and privilege to erect, establish, maintain and operate all buildings, machinery and works which the said party of the second part, their heirs, successors and assigns, may deem necessary, or may desire, for the manufacture and distribution of illuminating wood or coal gas, within Salt Lake City, to lay pipes under and along

[margin note: Use of streets.]

[margin note: Sole right for ten years.]

all and any of the streets, lanes and alleys of said City, in such manner and to such extent, within stated periods, as shall be hereinafter set forth, for the pur pose of distributing said gas throughout said City; and to sell said gas to all persons, corporations or associations within the said City desiring to purchase the same; and, generally, to have all rights and privileges, subject to the restrictions of these articles of agreement, necessary to the proper and successful prosecution of the business of making, distributing and selling illuminating gas in said Salt Lake City, it being understood, however, that the manufacture of gas by any person on his own premises for his private use is in no manner prohibited by this agreement.

And the said party of the first part doth hereby further covenant and agree to and with the said party of the second part, their heirs, successors and assigns, that they will not let, demise or grant, to any person, company or corporation, the right to establish gas-works within the corporate limits of said Salt Lake City; or to open, occupy or use any of the streets, lanes or alleys of said City for the purpose of laying pipes or other apparatus therein, for conveying, conducting or distributing gas, from the present time and until the complete expiration of a term of ten years from the eighth day of March, A. D., eighteen hundred and seventy-two (1872), unless the rights and privileges, which, by virtue of the said ordinance hereinbefore mentioned, have been. and by virtue of these articles of agreement, hereby are, granted to the said

Forfeit.   party of the second part, their heirs, successors and assigns, shall have become duly forfeited to the said party of the first part, as hereinafter provided.

And the said party of the first part doth hereby

further covenant and agree to and with the said party of the second part, their heirs, successors and assigns, that any person, company, or corporation, who may hereafter acquire or procure, from the said party of the first part, the right and privilege to establish gas-works, and to lay pipes in the streets of said Salt Lake City, for the purpose of conveying, conducting, or distributing gas, shall and will be restricted from lay- ing any of said pipes nearer than two and one half feet off the pipes then laid, or that may thereafter be laid by the said party of the second part, their heirs, suc- cessors or assigns, except where it may become neces- sary for said pipes to cross each other.

Other company pipes not nearer than 2½ feet.

And in consideration of the foregoing premises, covenants and agreements of the said party of the first part, the said party of the second part, do, for them- selves, their heirs, successors and assigns, hereby cove- nant and agree, to and with the said party of the first part, as follows, viz. : That within three months after the 30th day of March, A. D., eighteen hundred and seventy-two, the said party of the second part, their heirs, successors or assigns, will commence actual operations for the construction of the necessary works, for the said purpose of manufacturing, distributing and selling gas ; that on or before the eighth day of March, A. D., eighteen hundred and seventy-three (1873), the said gas-works shall be so far completed as to enable the said party of the second part, their heirs, succes- sors or assigns, to manufacture a good quality of il- luminating gas ; that at said last mentioned time, the said party of the second part, their heirs, successors or assigns, will have distributing pipes of sufficient capa- city laid, ready for use, from the point or place where the said gas is manufactured, in and through the streets being and lying within, and to the extent of the

When to be com- pleted.

following limits, to wit : South Temple to Third South

Street; east to Second East Street; north to Second North Street ; and west to Third West Street and place of beginning ; and be ready to furnish such gas, along the line of said pipes, to all the city street lamps that shall or may be erected within the limits above mentioned, and to all persons, bodies or associations within the said limits desiring to purchase and use the same. That, as soon thereafter as practicable, the said party of the second part, their heirs, successors or assigns, will lay pipes, distribute and sell gas, on any and all streets respectively of Salt Lake City, so far as there may be any reasonable demand for said gas on such streets, or as the said party of the first part, through its City

Council, may, from time to time, by resolution or ordinance, reasonably require said pipes to be extended. That the said party of the second part, their heirs, successors and assigns, will, at all times, be controlled and governed by the ordinance or ordinances of Salt Lake City then in force, relating to the manner of laying distributing pipes, and of making and guarding excavations therefor ; that the said party of the second

part, their heirs, successors or assigns, will be responsible for any damage, either to person or property, resulting from any act or negligence of theirs ; that said party of the second part, their heirs, successors or assigns, will, at all times, furnish a full and sufficient supply, to meet the demands thereof, of said illuminating gas, and of as good an average quality as is furnished to any city in any of the Territories of the United States, or Pacific States, unless prevented by accident or other cause beyond their control, in which event said obstacle shall be removed and overcome without unnecessary delay ; that said party of the second part, their heirs, successors and assigns, will,

at no time during the existence of these articles of
agreement, that is to say from the eighth day of March,
A. D., eighteen hundred and seventy-two (1872), for
and during the full term of twenty-one years thereafter, charge the inhabitants of said Salt Lake City a
price exceeding four dollars per one thousand cubic Price of gas.
feet for said gas, nor shall the price for supplying the
street lamps with said gas, and for the lighting, ex-
tinguishing, cleaning and keeping said lamps in proper
order and repair be in excess of sixty dollars per annum for each lamp, the party of the first part paying
for all necessary service pipes from mains to City lamp-
posts.

And the said party of the second part, their heirs,
successors and assigns, doth hereby further agree to
and with the said party of the first part, "for the purpose of reducing the price of gas," as follows, viz. :
That when the quantity of gas sold or consumed from
said gas-works in said Salt Lake City shall reach in
amount, or indicate the consumption of, one hundred
and twenty-five thousand (125,000) cubic feet per day,
the price of said gas shall be reduced fifty cents per Reduction of price of gas.
thousand, and from such date thereafter the price shall
not be in excess of three dollars and fifty cents per
thousand cubic feet ; and when the quantity of said gas
sold or consumed shall reach in amount, or indicate the
consumption of, one hundred and seventy-five thousand
(175,000) cubic feet per day, the price of said gas shall
again be reduced fifty cents per thousand. The price
of said gas to the inhabitants of said Salt Lake City
shall not be in excess of three dollars per one thousand
cubic feet, corresponding reduction in price to be made
for the City street lamps and City Hall. The said
party of the first part may appoint an examiner, who
shall, from time to time, have access to the books of

the said party of the second part, their heirs, successors and assigns, for the purpose of ascertaining the quantity of gas consumed.

And it is hereby further understood and agreed to, by and between the parties to these presents, that the rights and privileges which, by virtue of the said ordinance hereinbefore mentioned, have been, and which, by virtue of these articles of agreement hereby are, granted to the said party of the second part, their heirs, successors and assigns, are granted upon this express condition, anything herein contained to the contrary notwithstanding : that if the said party of the second part, their heirs, successors and assigns, shall not well and truly keep, perform and fulfil all and singular the covenants and agreements by them to be kept, performed and fulfilled, according to the true intent and meaning of these presents, then, and in that case, it shall and may be lawful for the said party of the first part, through its City Council, to annul this grant. And thereupon the franchise granted by virtue of said ordinance shall revert to the said party of the first part as fully and completely as if this agreement had never been executed, or said ordinance passed ; *Provided*, however, that before any action is taken to annul or vacate this grant, or any part thereof, the said party of the first part shall, through its City Council, cause a notice in writing to be served upon the said party of the second part, their heirs, successors or assigns, wh.ch said notice shall fully specify the covenant or article of agreement of which the said party of the second part, their heirs, successors or assigns, may be in default at the date of said notice.

And if, at the end of thirty days after the service of said notice, the said party of the second part, their heirs, successors or assigns, shall still be in default, or

Annulling grant.

Notice.

Default.

shall not have made satisfactory arrangements with the said party of the first part, for the performance or fulfilment of such covenant or article of agreement specified in said notice, then, and in that case, the City Council of said Salt Lake City may annul or vacate this grant, and by ordinance or resolution declare the rights and privileges granted by virtue of said ordinance to the said party of the second part, their heirs, successors and assigns, duly forfeited to the said party of the first part. *Forfeit.*

In witness of all which, the said party of the first part, by and through its Mayor, who hath been by the said party of the first part thereunto duly authorized, hath hereunto subscribed its corporate name, and affixed its common corporate seal. And,

In witness of all which, the said party of the second part, have hereunto set their hands and seals.

ARTICLE III.

Resolution Relating to Articles of Agreement.

Be it resolved by the City Council of Salt Lake City that the articles of agreement made by and between Salt Lake City, through the Mayor of said city, and P. Lalor Sherry, George A. Smith, Thomas W. Ellerbeck, James Jack and Thomas Williams, in relation to the establishment of gas works in Salt Lake City, be, and the same are, hereby approved, and the Mayor is hereby duly authorized to execute the same in behalf of said Salt Lake City, and to affix the corporate seal of said city thereto.

ARTICLE IV.

Resolution Approving the Location of the Salt Lake City Gas Company's Works, and for other purposes.

Be it resolved, by the City Council of Salt Lake City, that the location of the Salt Lake City Gas Company's Works, on lot one (1), in block eighty-two (82), plat A, Salt Lake City survey, be, and the same is, hereby approved.

Be it further resolved, that the Salt Lake City Gas Company have the privilege of constructing a railroad siding from said gas works, on lot one (1), block eighty-two (82), plat A, Salt Lake City survey, on or across Fourth West Street, upon a practicable curve, to connect, as short as possible, with the Utah Central Railroad.

And be it further resolved, that the said Salt Lake City Gas Company, be, and are, hereby granted the right to control and use the water issuing from a spring near the north-west corner of block eighty-three (83), plat A, Salt Lake City survey, with the privilege of conducting the same, (in pipes or otherwise) across Fourth West Street to the aforesaid Salt Lake City Company's gas works ; *Provided*: That these grants shall continue in force during the existence of the present Charter of the Salt Lake City Gas Company.

CHAPTER XV.

FOR THE PREVENTION OF FIRES.

SEC. 1. Be it ordained by the City Council of Great Salt Lake City, that no person shall set off any fireworks, set up any stove, furnace or other apparatus in which fire is to be kept, or carry fire in the streets, without observing the following regulations, under penalty of not less than one nor more than one hundred dollars for each offence.

SEC. 2. No person shall be allowed within the limits of the City to discharge or set off any rocket, squib, cracker or other fireworks without the consent of the Mayor, specifying the time when and the place where the same may be done.

SEC. 3. No stove or other apparatus in which fire is to be kept shall be set nearer than eight inches from the floor except such as have no fireplace on the lower plate; such can be set within four inches of the floor on which they stand; and the top and the side plates thereof shall not be set nearer than twelve inches off any wood partition, or other wood-work without protecting the same effectually from fire, by a metal lie, or other covering; and no pipe belonging thereto shall be put up, unless it shall be conducted into a chimney made of brick, stone or other incombustible material, or if passing through the woodwork

No pipe near wood-work.

or roof of a building, there shall be a space of not less than four inches between the pipe and the wood, and the pipe shall be kept from nearer contact with the wood by some safe material, and shall project four feet above or beyond the roof or wood-work; *Provided*, the Mayor or any alderman shall deem the above to be equally safe, then to be certified under his hand.

SEC. 4. No person shall be allowed to carry or cause to be carried in any street, thoroughfare or lot of this city, any burning coals or brand of fire, unless the same be in a covered vessel.

No fire to be carried through streets.

SEC. 5. All forge and furnace chimneys or flues shall be raised at least four feet above the roof, by or through which they pass and shall have a deadening flue, or fire spark arrester of wove wire placed on the top or within such chimney or flue.

SEC. 6. The owner or occupant of any house, shop or other building shall cause the flues or chimneys thereof to be swept or burnt out as often as may be required to keep the same cleaned. In case of burning out flues, it shall de done in the day time, and only when the roof and other surrounding combustibles are wet. Any person suffering the flues of any house occupied by him or her to become foul and take fire, or be fired, at any other time than herein specified, shall be liable to the penalties prescribed in the first section of this ordinance.

Chimneys to be cleaned.

SEC. 7. It shall be the duty of the Inspector of Buildings to examine carefully, under the direction of the City Council, any cause from which immediate danger of fire may be apprehended, and remove or abate, with the consent of the Mayor or any Alderman

Duty of Inspector of Buildings.

(in case of neglect or refusal of the owner or occupant) any cause from which danger may be apprehended, and to cause all buildings, chimneys, stoves, pipes, hearths, ovens, boilers, ash-houses, and other apparatus used in any building which shall be found in such condition as to be considered unsafe, to be, without delay, at the expense of the owner or occupant thereof, put in such condition as not to be dangerous in causing or promoting fires.

SEC. 8. If any person shall obstruct or hinder any person under the direction of the Inspector of Buildings aforesaid in the performance of his duty, under the preceding section, such person for every such offence shall forfeit and pay the penalty of twenty-five dollars.

————o————

CHAPTER XVI.

FIRE DEPARTMENT.

SEC. 1. Be it ordained by the City Council of Salt Lake City, that there is created the office of Chief Engineer of the Fire Department of said City, which office shall be filled by appointment of the City Council. Said Engineer may appoint one or more assistants, who shall take command in his absence.

Chief Engineer.

SEC. 2. There is authorized the formation of an Engine Company in said City, to be known by the name of "Engine Company No. 1," which shall be composed of fifty able-bodied men, residents of said City, *viz.* : A Foreman, Assistant Foreman, Secretary, Treasurer, Steward, and forty-five members, whose duty it shall be to keep their engine and implements, in good order and ready for use; and, on the alarm of fire, they are hereby required to leave all other business and repair to the engine house, with all possible speed, and remove their engine to the place of fire, and operate under the direction of the Chief Engineer or assistant.

Duty of members.

SEC. 3. There may be organized in said City, a hook and ladder company, to be known by the name of "Hook and Ladder Company, No. 1," which shall be composed of thirty able-bodied men, residents of said City, *viz.* : A Foreman, Assistant Foreman, Secretary, Treasurer, Steward and twenty-five members, whose duty it shall be to keep their implements in good order and ready for use ; and on the alarm of fire they are hereby required to remove their implements to the place of fire, and do duty under the direction of the aforesaid Chief Engineer, or assistant.

Hook and Ladder Company.

SEC. 4. The Chief Engineer is hereby authorized to enlist eighty men, to compose the companies hereinbefore provided for, who shall proceed to elect their officers by ballot, from their own number, under his direction, and they shall adopt such rules and regulations as may be deemed necessary. And it shall further be the duty of said Engineer, together with his assistants to take charge and command of all fire, hose and hook and ladder companies, with their engines and implements, in all places and under all circumstances in said City, and provide, or cause to be provided,

Rules and duties.

engines and other implements used for the extinguishment of fires, under the direction of the City Council, and see that they are kept in good order.

SEC. 5. The Chief Engineer and all officers of said companies, before entering upon the duties of their respective offices, shall be sworn before the City Recorder, faithfully to perform the duties thereof. The Chief Engineer and assistants shall give bonds with securities in the penal sum of five thousand dollars each, which shall be approved by and filed with the City Recorder. All vacancies that may occur from death, resignation, removal, or otherwise, in said companies, shall be filled by a majority vote of the officers and members present at any regular meeting. *Officers give bonds.*

SEC. 6. The said Chief Engineer is hereby empowered to organize other companies when it shall be deemed necessary, under the direction of the City Council, to whom he shall make a quarterly report; and the Secretary of each company shall make quarterly reports to the Chief Engineer; and all acts and doings of said Chief Engineer and fire companies shall be subject to the approval of said Council. *Reports.*

SEC. 7. In case of fire, the signal shall be, one stroke of City Hall bell for north, two for south, three for east, and four for west of said Hall. *Signals.*

SEC. 8. The names and places of residence of the Engineers, Officers and members of each company shall be posted up in the police station by the Secretary of the same, the first week in January of each year. Whenever any fire shall happen in the night, the policeman on duty at the City Hall shall ring the alarm, and the police night watch shall give notice to *Night watch.*

the Engineer, Officers or Firemen nearest the Engine House, and alarm the citizens by the cry of fire, mentioning the street where it may be known.

———o———

CHAPTER XVII.

RESOLUTION IN RELATION TO SMALLPOX.

Be it resolved by the City Council of Salt Lake City that, in view of the probability of the City being infected with the smallpox, the Quarantine Physicians are hereby ordered to immediately quarantine or isolate every case reported to and decided by them to be smallpox, or varioloid ; and are hereby authorized to make and enforce any regulations necessary in the premises. In case of neglect or refusal on the part of any person to comply with the requirement of the law in reference to removal, or otherwise, upon the report of the physicians to that effect to the Mayor or any Alderman, the said Mayor or Alderman shall issue an order to the City Marshal, who shall immediately call to his aid the necessary assistance and proceed to carry out the requirement of the law.

[marginal note: Isolating every case.]

CHAPTER XVIII.

IN RELATION TO QUARANTINE.

SEC. 1. Be it ordained by the City Council of Salt Lake City, that said City and all that district of country embraced within twelve miles of the outer limits thereof, be, and the same are, hereby declared subject to quarantine regulations.

SEC. 2. The City Council shall appoint one or more quarantine physicians, each of whom, before entering upon the duties of his office, shall take and subscribe an oath, and give bonds in the penal sum of five thousand dollars, conditioned for the faithful performance thereof, who, associated with the Mayor, shall constitute a Board of Quarantine, and whose duty it shall be to make and enforce quarantine regulations within the above described quarantine limits. *Board of Quarantine.*

SEC. 3. That if any person or persons shall be found in an unhealthy condition from any contagious disease, within the aforesaid quarantine limits, they shall, if in the judgment of said Board of Quarantine the safety of the person so infected, or the public, shall render such action necessary, be required to remove forthwith to such place, within said limits as said Board may direct; and if any such person shall neglect or refuse to comply therewith, it shall be the duty of said Board to have it done at the expense of *Contagious disease.*

H

said person; and if in the judgment of said Board it shall be deemed advisable for the person so infected to remain in his usual place of abode for care and treatment, the said Board shall compel the strict quarantining of said place of abode, by causing to be kept displayed conspicuously during the period of danger a yellow flag upon such premises, as well as by establishing a guard at, or near the same; by giving notice in the most public manner practicable that said premises are infected; and, further, by regulating and prohibiting ingress and egress to and from said premises, until all danger from infection therein shall have ceased, and the most thorough measures for disinfecting said premises shall have been taken. And if the effects of any person be found in a condition liable to engender contagious disease, the same shall, at the discretion of the quarantine physician, be removed or destroyed at the expense of the owner thereof; and in the event of the removal of any person so infected, the premises from which he is removed, and the household thus exposed, shall be strictly quarantined until all danger of infection shall have passed; and such measures for the purification of said premises shall be taken as in the judgment of the quarantine physicians shall be necessary.

SEC. 4. The names of all quarantine physicians shall be published in some newspaper printed in Salt Lake City, during the continuance of the contagion. All physicians or other persons having any knowledge of the existence of any malignant contagious disease, or having reason to believe any such disease exists, are hereby required to report the same forthwith to a quarantine physician; and physicians, nurses, or any other persons who have been or shall be exposed to

[margin: Yellow flag.]

[margin: Disinfecting.]

[margin: Reporting cases.]

such contagious disease, are hereby forbidden to mingle with or be in the presence of others subject to the contagion, in such clothing as may have been used where there was such disease, or otherwise expose any person to such contagion.

SEC. 5. Any person neglecting or refusing to comply with the above requirements shall be liable to a fine not exceeding one hundred dollars, or be imprisoned not to exceed six months, or both fine and imprisonment. *Refusal.*

SEC. 6. That an ordinance entitled "An Ordinance regulating Quarantine" passed March 12th, 1850, and an ordinance entitled, "An Ordinance in relation to Quarantine," passed July 28th, 1871, be, and the same are, hereby repealed.

— ·——o——

CHAPTER XIX.

RELATING TO PAWNBROKERS.

SEC. 1. Be it ordained by the City Council of Salt Lake City, that all persons before receiving license as pawnbrokers shall produce, to the Mayor or City Council, satisfactory evidence of their good character to engage in or carry on such business.

SEC. 2. Every person so licensed shall, at the time of receiving such license, give bonds with two

sureties, to the acceptance of the City Recorder, in
the sum of one thousand dollars, conditioned for the
due observance of all ordinances passed by the City
Council, or in force respecting pawnbrokers, at any
time during the continuance of such license, and shall
keep posted up in his place of business a copy of all
ordinances relating to pawnbrokers.

SEC. 3.   Every pawnbroker shall keep a book, in
which shall be fairly written, at the time of each loan,
an accurate account and description of the goods,
article or thing pawned, the amount of money loaned
thereon, the time of the pledging of the same, the rate
of interest to be paid on such loan, and the name and
residence of the person pawning or pledging the said
goods, article or thing.

SEC. 4.   Every pawnbroker shall, at the time of
each loan, deliver to the person pawning or pledging
any goods, article or thing, a memorandum or note
signed by him, containing the substance of the entry
required to be made in his book by the last preceding
section, and no charge shall be made or received by
any pawnbroker for any such entry, memorandum or
note.

SEC. 5.   The said book shall, at all reasonable
times, be open to the inspection of the Mayor, Recorder
or Aldermen of the City, or of any person who shall
be duly authorized in writing for that purpose, by
either of them, and who shall exhibit such written
authority to such pawnbrokers.

SEC. 6. Every pawnbroker who shall violate, or
neglect, or refuse to comply with any or either of the
provisions of the second, third, fourth, or fifth sections

of this ordinance, shall, on conviction thereof, be liable to a fine in any sum not exceeding fifty dollars for every such offence.

SEC. 7. No pawnbroker shall ask, demand, or receive any greater rate of interest than forty per cent. per annum, upon any loan not exceeding the sum of twenty-five dollars, or, than twenty-four per cent. per annum upon any loan exceeding the sum of twenty-five dollars, under the penalty of one hundred dollars for every such offence. *Rate to be charged.*

SEC. 8. No pawnbroker shall sell any pawn or pledge until the same shall have remained one year in his possession, and all such sales shall be at public auction and not otherwise, and shall be made or conducted by such auctioneer as shall be approved of, for that purpose, by the Mayor. *Sale of pawns.*

SEC. 9. Notice of every such sale shall be published, for at least ten consecutive days previous thereto, in one or more of the daily newspapers having general circulation, printed in Salt Lake City; and such notice shall specify the time and place at which such sale is to take place, the name of the auctioneer by whom the sale is to be conducted, and a description of the goods or articles to be sold. *Notice of sale.*

SEC. 10. The surplus money, if any, arising from such sale, after deducting the amount of the loan and the interest then due on the same, shall be paid over by the pawnbroker to the person who would be entitled to redeem the pledge in case no such sale had taken place. *Surplus money.*

SEC. 11. No pawnbroker shall, under any pretence whatever, purchase or buy any second-hand furniture, metals or clothes, or any other article, or thing whatever, offered to him as a pawn or pledge.

SEC. 12. No pawnbroker shall receive any goods, article, or thing, in pawn or pledge, of a person who is intoxicated, and known to be an habitual drunkard, a thief, or an insane person; or on being notified in writing by any responsible person of the character, habits or condition of such person or persons; nor shall said pawnbroker receive a pawn or pledge of any person under fourteen years of age.

From whom to take nothing in pawn.

SEC. 13. Every pawnbroker who shall violate, or neglect, or refuse to comply with, either of the provisions of the eighth, ninth, tenth, eleventh, and twelfth sections of this ordinance, shall, for every such offence, forfeit and pay a sum not exceeding one hundred dollars into the City Treasury.

———o———

CHAPTER XX.

REGULATING AUCTIONEERS.

———

SEC. 1. Be it ordained by the City Council of Salt Lake City, that no person shall be allowed to sell or expose for sale, by way of vendue, or auction, any property within the limits of said city, without first obtaining a license from said Council for such purpose; for which such person shall pay into the City Treasury

Price of license.

the sum of one per cent. of all moneys received on all
goods sold by him, and give bonds to said city, with Bonds.
approved securities, in the sum of one thousand dollars, conditioned for the honest and due performance
of all duties as herein required, which bonds shall be
approved by and filed in the office of the City Recorder.

SEC. 2. That all auctioneers so licensed shall receive all articles which they may be required to sell at
auction, and give receipts for the same; and at the close
of any sale shall deliver a fair account of such sale Commis-
and pay the amount received for such articles to the sion.
person or persons entitled thereto, deducting therefrom
a commission not to exceed ten per cent. on the amount
of such sales.

SEC. 3. It shall be the duty of every auctioneer,
licensed as aforesaid, to pay the sum of one per
cent. into the City Treasury on all sums realized on
all goods or chattels by him sold, monthly, or oftener
if required; and in accounting for such sales it shall Sworn re-
be incumbent on every auctioneer to make his returns turns.
under oath or affirmation, and exhibit to the City Recorder his books of sales when required so to do by
said recorder; and should any auctioneer neglect or
refuse to comply with the foregoing requirements, he
shall forfeit his license, and be liable to pay a fine in
any sum not less than ten nor more than one hundred
dollars for each offence.

SEC. 4. All auctioneers are hereby forbidden
to sell, or expose for sale, any kind of property so near Obstruct-
the streets as to cause people to gather in crowds on ing street.
the sidewalks so as to obstruct the same, or to use im-
moral or indecent language in crying their goods, or to

make noisy acclamations or ring bells through the
streets in advertising their goods or chattels.

Sheriff's
auction.

Sec. 5. Nothing in this ordinance shall be so
construed as to prohibit any sheriff, constable, or other
officer, whose duty shall require him to sell property
at public auction from so doing.

Fine.

Sec. 6. Any person violating any of the provisions of this ordinance, when not otherwise provided for,
shall be liable to a fine in any sum not less than one
nor more than one hundred dollars for each offence.

Repeal.

Sec. 7. That the ordinance entitled "An Ordinance regulating Auctioneers and Commission Merchants," passed March 17th, 1860, is hereby repealed.

———o———

CHAPTER XXI.

RELATING TO DOGS.

Tax.

Sec. 1. Be it ordained by the City Council of
Salt Lake City, that it shall not be lawful for any
person to own or keep a dog within the limits of this
City, without making application to the City Recorder
for that purpose, and shall pay to said Recorder, for
the benefit of the City, an annual tax of three dollars.
The Recorder shall register the applicant's name and a
description of the dog, and give to said applicant a
certificate of registry. Any person found violating
this section shall be liable to a fine in any sum not

less than three nor more than ten dollars for each offence.

SEC. 2. All dogs so registered shall wear a suitable collar with the owner's name or initials of the same inscribed thereon, together with the number cor- Collar. responding with the certificate of registry, and all dogs found at large not registered and collared as aforesaid shall be liable to be killed by any person.

SEC. 3. Any female dog found running at large while in heat shall be liable to be killed, and the Female dog. owner or possessor thereof to a fine in any sum not exceeding fifteen dollars.

SEC. 4. Any owner or possessor of a dog permitting or suffering the same to enter or be in any Place of worship. place of worship during public service, shall be liable to a fine in any sum not exceeding five dollars for each offence.

SEC. 5. If any owner or possessor of a fierce, dangerous or mischievous dog, permit the same to go Fierce dog. at large, he shall be liable to be fined for the first offence in the sum of five dollars; for the second offence the sum of ten dollars; and upon the third conviction for the like offence shall pay fifteen dollars, and the city marshal shall immediately cause said dog to be killed. The said marshal is hereby authorized to cause the destruction of all dogs not registered according to the provisions of this ordinance.

SEC. 6. Any person who shall kill, or cause to be killed, any dog registered as provided in this Registered dog not to ordinance, without the consent of the owner, or pos- be killed. sessor thereof, or deprive a registered dog of its collar, or put a collar on any dog not registered, shall be liable to a fine in any sum not exceeding twenty-five dollars.

SEC. 7. This ordinance shall take effect from and after the first day of April next.

SEC. 8. "An ordinance relating to dogs" passed April 27th, 1860, be and the same is hereby repealed.

————o————

CHAPTER XXII.

MODE OF PROCEDURE IN CASES ARISING UNDER CITY ORDINANCES.

———

SEC. 1. Be it ordained by the City Council of Salt Lake City, that whenever a complaint is made before the Mayor or an Alderman of said City, on oath or affirmation; or if the Mayor or Alderman has personal knowledge that a breach of the ordinances of the city has been committed, he shall forthwith issue a warrant, directed to the Marshal, commanding him or any of his deputies to arrest the accused and bring him or them forthwith before said Mayor or Alderman for examination or trial.

Issue warrant.

SEC. 2. Any peace officer of the City witnessing any breach of the ordinances shall arrest the offender, or cause it to be done, with or without process, and bring him before the Mayor or an Alderman, to be

Peace officers arrest.

dealt with according to the provisions of the ordinances without unnecessary delay.

SEC. 3. Any person may arrest another in the commission of an offence against the ordinances of said city, and must, without unnecessary delay, take the offender before the Mayor, or one of the Aldermen, or deliver him to the nearest peace officer of said city. *Any person may arrest.*

SEC. 4. When any person shall be brought before the Mayor or an Alderman, charged with the commission of an offence, such person shall be examined or tried without unnecessary delay; *Provided*: That when necessary such person may be detained in the city prison not to exceed forty-eight hours before trial. *Detention.*

SEC. 5. The Court shall issue subpœnas, directed to the proper officer, for the witnesses, if required, and shall forthwith proceed to hear the evidence, and determine upon the complaint alleged; *Provided*: That neither party shall have more than three witnesses to prove any one fact, except at his own expense, and that complaint in writing shall not be necessary, unless demanded by the defence. *Witnesses limited.*

SEC. 6. Upon good cause shown, the Court may postpone the trial, and shall require the defendant to enter into recognizance with sufficient security, to appear at such time as the Court may determine, to answer the complaint made against him. If he fail to give such security, he shall be held in custody, or be committed to prison until the time of trial. *Recognizance.*

SEC. 7. The defendant on being brought before the Court, shall be informed of the charge preferred against him, or the complaint when made in writing

shall be read, and he shall be enquired of, whether guilty or not guilty. If he plead guilty the Court may enquire into the extent of guilt and render judg-
Pleading. ment; if he plead not guilty, or refuses to answer, the evidence on the part of the prosecution shall be heard, then that of the defence ; after which, if either party can satisfy the Court that important evidence which he can procure is still wanting, reasonable time may be granted to procure such evidence. When all the evidence is heard, the prosecution and defense may make such applicable remarks as shall be deemed proper, and the Court shall render judgment as soon as practicable..

SEC. 8. The Court shall keep a docket-book, in **Docket.** which shall be entered the title and nature of the complaint, the names of the witnesses who testified in the case, the proceedings thereon and the judgment of the Court.

SEC. 9. If the defendant fails to pay the fine and costs awarded in the judgment against him, the Court shall issue an execution against the defendant, com-
Imprison-ment at labor. mitting him to imprisonment at labor, either with or without a ball and chain attached to his person ; *Provided* : That property may be delivered by the defendant, or the same may be taken by the officer, in sufficient quantity to satisfy said execution, which shall be disposed of as hereinafter directed.

SEC. 10. When property is delivered or taken to satisfy a judgment, the Marshal shall give public notice of time and place of sale, and description of the kind of property to be sold, allowing ten days from the levy of execution to the day of sale, unless the interest of the defendant shall require a shorter time, and shall sell the same, or so much thereof as may be Returns of necessary, and make returns within five days from the sale. day of sale, and pay over to the Court the proceeds arising therefrom, and the excess if any shall be paid over to the defendant, and all fines collected by the Mayor or Alderman, shall be paid into the City Treasury, monthly, or oftener if required.

SEC. 11. If required by either party, the Court shall issue a *venire*, requiring the Marshal, or deputy, to summon six competent persons, or a less number if agreed upon by the parties, to serve as jurors, who may be objected to for cause; *Provided* : That either party shall be entitled to three peremptory challenges. Challeng-If any are removed, their places shall be filled; and es. when the number is complete, they shall be sworn to give a just verdict, according to the law and evidence, and to have no communication with any but the Court personally, or through the officer, or with a fellow juror, in reference to the case before them, until they have agreed upon a verdict, or been dis- Verdict. charged. The Court may direct the jury to bring in a sealed verdict in case of an agreement during a recess.

SEC. 12. Upon complaint being made in writing and under oath, before the Mayor or any Alderman, Threats. that any person has threatened to commit an offence against the person or property of another, said Mayor or Alderman may issue a warrant, reciting the substance of the complaint, commanding the Marshal or any of his deputies, forthwith to bring the person so charged before him to answer said complaint, and if, on examination, the court is satisfied from the testimony that there are sufficient grounds to fear such an offence will be committed by the person complained of, he shall require the offender to enter into recognizance in any sum not exceeding one thousand dollars to keep the peace towards the people of said city, and particularly toward the complainant, for a term not exceeding six months. If the offender fail to give bonds with securities when required, he may be imprisoned until he give such bonds, not, however, exceeding sixty days.

Penalty.

SEC. 13. Whenever a complaint shall be made before the Mayor, or any Alderman, in writing and under oath, of property having been stolen or embezzled, and that he believes such property to be concealed in any house, or place (describing the property and place) within the limits of said city, and the Mayor or Alderman is satisfied that there is reasonable ground for such belief, he shall issue a warrant commanding the Marshal or any of his deputies to search diligently the house or place where such property is believed to be secreted, and said Marshal shall make returns of his doings without delay; and all property recovered under such process shall be subject to the order of the court.

Search for stolen property.

SEC. 14. Persons taken into custody, charged with larceny, shall be liable to be searched by the officer making the arrest, for money or other property described in the complaint, and if found the same may be taken and held subject to the order of the court, and persons arrested for any offence may be disarmed.

Search of person.

SEC. 15. The Mayor is authorized to issue his proclamation offering a reward of such an amount as he, in his discretion, may deem proper for the arrest, and delivery to the proper officer, of any person who may

Reward.

be charged with crime committed within the city, whenever he shall have knowledge of such occurrence or receive information in relation thereto from any responsible person or persons.

SEC. 16. All criminal prosecutions arising under the ordinances of this city, must be commenced and carried on in the name of Salt Lake City.

————o————

CHAPTER XXIII.

IN RELATION TO THE SELLING OF FRESH MEATS.

SEC. 1. Be it ordained by the City Council of Salt Lake City, that it shall not be lawful for any person to carry on the business of selling fresh meats within the limits of said City, without first obtaining a license therefor. *License to be obtained.*

SEC. 2. All applications for license to carry on the business of selling fresh meats shall be made to the Mayor in writing, who is hereby authorized to grant such licenses on payment into the City Treasury of the sum of fifty dollars per annum, payable in advance. Said application shall specify where the business is to be carried on. *Price of license.*

SEC. 3. In the license to sell fresh meats it shall be stated where the business is to be carried on; but such license shall not authorize such business to be *Place of business.*

carried on at any place other than as therein designated. Such license shall not be transferable, nor shall authorize any person to carry on such business other than as named therein.

SEC. 4. Licenses granted under this ordinance may be issued for three months, *pro rata*, with fifteen per cent. additional, and for six months, *pro rata*, with ten per cent. additional.

Term of license.

SEC. 5. Any persons refusing or neglecting to comply with the provisions of this ordinance, shall be liable to a fine not exceeding one hundred dollars, and to imprisonment not exceeding six months, for every such offence.

Fine.

———o———

CHAPTER XXIV.

RELATING TO BUTCHERING AND SLAUGHTER-HOUSES.

SEC. 1. Be it ordained by the City Council of Salt Lake City, that it shall not be lawful for any person or persons to erect any slaughter-house or yard, or engage in the business of butchering within the limits of said city without first obtaining license therefor, nor at any place or places other than such as may be designated by said council.

License.

SEC. 2. Applications for license, under the provisions of this ordinance, shall be made to the Mayor in writing, and licenses shall be issued and signed by the Mayor or presiding officer of the City Council, and attested by the City Recorder, under the corporate seal, on the payment into the City Treasury of the sum of twenty-five dollars per annum, in advance. Price of license.

SEC. 3. All persons licensed as butchers shall keep a book in which they shall record a faithful description of the age, size and color of all animals by them killed, with the brands and ear-marks thereon, together with the name of the person from whom received and the time when killed; which book shall be open to the inspection of the public. Record.

SEC. 4. All persons engaged in the business of butchering within the limits of this city are hereby required to thoroughly cleanse their slaughter-houses and yards, once each twenty-four hours, and to remove from their premises and deposit all offal in such manner and at such place or places as may be designated by the City Marshal, or his deputy. Cleansing.

SEC. 5. It shall be the duty of the City Marshal or his deputy (as often as may be deemed necessary) to visit the slaughter-houses within the limits of this city, to examine the books and see that a faithful record is made of all animals killed, and that the slaughter-houses are thoroughly cleansed, as provided in section four of this ordinance. Examining books.

SEC. 6. Any person violating the provisions of this ordinance shall be liable to a fine in any sum not less than five, nor more than one hundred, dollars, and on a second conviction in addition thereto his license may be declared forfeited. Fine.

SEC. 7. All ordinances or parts of ordinances conflicting with this ordinance are hereby repealed.

I

CHAPTER XXV.

ESTABLISHING A MARKET IN THE SECOND MARKET DIS-
TRICT IN SALT LAKE CITY AND FOR OTHER
PURPOSES.

Be it resolved, by the City Council of Salt Lake
City, that a Market is hereby established in the Second
Market District, in accordance with the provisions of
an Ordinance, entitled "An Ordinance in relation to
Markets and Market Masters," passed August 21, 1871,
and that until Markets shall be established in the other
Market Districts, all rules and regulations of the City
concerning Markets are, and shall be considered,
equally in force therein.

————o————

CHAPTER XXVI.

ESTABLISHING A MARKET IN THE FIFTH MARKET DIS-
TRICT IN SALT LAKE CITY.

Be it resolved, by the City Council of Salt Lake
City, that a market be and is hereby established in
the Fifth Market District, in accordance with the
provisions of an ordinance, entitled "An Ordinance in
relation to Markets and Market Masters," passed
August 21st, 1871.

CHAPTER XXVII.

IN RELATION TO NUISANCES.

SEC. 1. Be it ordained, by the City Council of Salt Lake City, that no person shall have, make, use or keep, at any place within the corporate limits of Salt Lake City, any noisome, offensive or unwholesome substance, or any vat, pit or pool of standing water, whether for tanner's, skinner's, dresser's, or other use ; nor shall any person have a pig-stye, cow-house, shed, stable or privy, or suffer any offal or other refuse matter from the same to accumulate on their premises, which may cause any noisome, offensive or unwholesome smell. *Offensive substance.*

SEC. 2. No person shall be allowed to stack or pile any hay, oats, straw, wheat or other combustible matter nearer than fifty feet to any dwelling-house or other place where fire is used. *Combustibles.*

SEC. 3. No person shall cast, or leave, or keep in or adjoining any street, lane, avenue, alley, square, public place, road, or any yard, lot, field or premises in said City, any bones, putrid, unsound, unwholesome or refuse meat of any animal, or any unsound fish, hides or skins of any kind, or the whole or any part of any dead animal or animals, or any other unsound, putrid, or unwholesome substances, garbage, or offensive or useless parts of any beeves, calves, sheep, *Filth on streets.*

hogs or cattle, or any offal, garbage or filth from any house, out-house, stable, shop, store, hotel, restaurant, or other place.

Tanners, etc. SEC. 4. No tanner, skinner, butcher or vendor of fish or meats, or other person, shall bring to or keep, for the period of twenty-four hours in any part of said City, any undressed or uncurried hide, skin or leather, or any other materials whatever, which may cause any noisome, offensive or unwholesome smell. All things specified as offensive in this ordinance are hereby declared to be nuisances.

Fine. SEC. 5. Any person violating any of the provisions of this ordinance shall, on conviction therefor, be fined in any sum not exceeding fifty dollars for the first offence, and adjudged to abate or remove forthwith from said City the offensive matter with which he may be charged ; and for any second or subsequent offence a fine of one hundred dollars, or imprisonment for six months, or both fine and imprisonment at the discretion of the court, and the said nuisance may be abated or removed by the city authorities at the expense of the accused.

Repealed. SEC. 6. All ordinances and parts of ordinances heretofore passed relating to nuisances, inconsistent with the provisions of this ordinance, are hereby repealed.

CHAPTER XXVIII.

REGULATING CELLAR-WAYS ON THE SIDE-WALKS.

SEC. 1. Be it ordained by the City Council of Salt Lake City that cellar-ways, or entrances to the basement of buildings on the side-walks of this City, may Width. be constructed not to exceed five feet in width, and running parallel with the building on the line of the lots; said entrances to be protected by iron railings and gates not less than three feet high, subject to the approval of the Street Supervisor; the owners of such Responsible. property being responsible for damages accruing from accidents resulting therefrom.

SEC. 2. All entrances to basements heretofore established or constructed, must within sixty days be made to conform to the requirements of this ordi- Conform. nance.

SEC. 3. Any person refusing or neglecting to comply with the provisions of this ordinance, shall be Fine. liable to a fine not exceeding one hundred dollars.

CHAPTER XXIX.

DIVIDING SALT LAKE CITY INTO MUNICIPAL WARDS.

SEC. 1. Be it ordained by the City Council of Salt Lake City, that the City be, and the same is, hereby divided into five Municipal Wards, described and bounded as follows, to wit:

All that portion of the corporate limits lying south of the centre of Third South Street, extending to the east boundary of the City, and east of the centre of East Temple Street, extending to the south boundary of the city, shall constitute the First Ward.

Locationof 1st Ward.

All that portion of the corporate limits lying west of the centre of East Temple Street, extending to the south boundary of the city and south of the centre of South Temple Street, extending to the west boundary of the city, shall constitute the Second Ward.

Locationof 2nd Ward.

All that portion of the corporate limits lying north of the centre of South Temple Street, extending to the west boundary of the city and west of the centre of East Temple Street, extending to the north boundary of the city, shall constitute the Third Ward.

Locationof 3rd Ward.

All that portion of the corporate limits lying north of the centre of South Temple Street, extending to the east boundary of the city and east of the centre of East Temple Street, extending to

Locationof 4th Ward.

the north boundary of the city, shall constitute the Fourth Ward.

All that portion of the corporate limits lying east of the centre of East Temple Street, between the centre of South Temple Street and the centre of Third South Street, extending to the east boundary of the city, shall constitute the Fifth Ward. Location of 5th Ward.

SEC. 2. An ordinance, entitled, "An Ordinance dividing the city into Wards," passed February 29th, 1860, be, and the same is, hereby repealed. Repealed.

————o————

CHAPTER XXX.

AUTHORIZING THE SURVEY AND A PLAT TO BE FILED IN THE OFFICE OF THE CITY RECORDER OF A CERTAIN PIECE OR PARCEL OF LAND TO BE CALLED HEREAFTER PLAT I AND FOR OTHER PURPOSES.

————

Be it resolved, by the City Council of Salt Lake City, that the City Surveyor proceed to survey and plat a tract or parcel of land, to be called hereafter Plat I, commencing at a point eight (8) rods north and two (2) rods west from the north-west corner of Block seventy-four (74) Plat A, thence east to the west line of Plat D, thence north to the north line of section 31, thence west to the east line of the Arsenal Grounds, thence southerly to the place of beginning ; including on said Plat the line of the City Water Works, so far Location.

as the same shall cross said described grounds, the right of way for said water works to be secured to said City by the proprietors of said plat of ground ; said survey to be named Plat I and to be filed in the office of the City Recorder.

————o————

CHAPTER XXXI.

IN RELATION TO ORNAMENTING THE STREETS.

————

Be it resolved, by the City Council of Salt Lake City, that lot-owners residing. on opposite blocks on any of the streets of said City, that are eight rods in width, are hereby granted the privilege of ornamenting said streets opposite their premises by occupying twenty-four feet of the centre thereof, with trees, shrubbery, lawns, flowers, etc., and protecting the same ; the nature or extent of the aforenamed improvements to be submitted to the Committee on Streets and Alleys for their approval and to be under their direction.

CHAPTER XXXII.

IN RELATION TO OBSTRUCTIONS UPON THE STREETS AND SIDE-WALKS.

SEC. 1. Be it ordained, by the City Council of Salt Lake City, that every owner or occupant of a lot is hereby required to remove from the street, and side-walk fronting the same, wagons, lumber, wood, boxes, fencing or other obstructions ; and any person who shall obstruct any of the side-walks, streets or alleys, except by permission of the City Council, shall be liable to a fine of not less than one nor more than fifty dollars for each offence. *Remove obstruction.*

SEC. 2. All persons driving a team, or leading, riding or driving any animal upon any side-walk in this City, shall be liable for all damages accruing thereby, and a fine of not less than one, nor more than fifty dollars for every such offence. *Provided* nothing in this section shall be so construed as to prohibit persons from crossing the sidewalk to or from their premises with teams or animals. *Animals on side-walks.*

SEC. 3. All persons are hereby forbidden to obstruct the sidewalks or streets by games of any kind, playing at ball, quoits, marbles, jumping, rolling of hoops, flying of kites, to annoy or obstruct the free travel of any footpassenger or team, under the penalty *Games.*

K

Fine.

of not less than one, nor more than fifty dollars, or imprisonment not to exceed twenty days, or both, for each offence, and to pay all damages.

———o———

CHAPTER XXXIII.

IN RELATION TO WATER, WATER-DITCHES
AND CULVERTS.

———

Suitable
ditches.

SEC. 1.   Be it ordained by the City Council of Salt Lake City, that all owners or occupants of lots in said City, requiring water from a main ditch for irrigation or other purposes, are hereby authorized and required to dig suitable ditches to convey the water across the side-walks, to or from their respective lots.

Box cul-
verts.

SEC. 2.   All persons having ditches across the side-walks to or from their respective lots, are hereby required to make good box culverts and keep them in repair, the covering of the culverts to be on the same grade as the side-walks, and to put suitable watertight gates at the ditch entrances of the culverts ; and when their times for irrigating expire they shall securely close said gates.

Allot-
ment.

SEC. 3.   All persons using ditch water on their lots, during the period when it is allotted by the water-masters, and after official notice of said allotment, at any time or in any quantity not so allotted, shall be liable to a fine of not less than one nor more than fifty dollars.

SEC. 4. All persons having ditches running in front of their lots, between the street and sidewalk, or having ditches in their lots, are hereby required to so fix said ditches that the water shall not flow therefrom to the injury of said streets or sidewalks, or to the waste of said water during any period of its allotment for irrigation.

Overflowing.

SEC. 5. All persons desiring to place dams or sluiceways in the water-ditches, are hereby required to obtain permission from and construct them under the direction of the water-master having jurisdiction, and to keep them in proper order, as provided for in the fourth section of this ordinance.

Sluiceways.

SEC. 6. All owners of city lots, or parts of city lots or farming lands, within the limits of said City, are hereby required to make and keep in repair the ditches opposite their lots, or parts of lots or farming lands.

Ditches to be kept in repair.

SEC. 7. When it is necessary to make and repair ditches, to convey water for irrigation or other purposes it shall be the duty of the water-master to give to the persons concerned therein reasonable notice of the time and place such work is to be done; and it shall be the duty of such persons to make their proportions of said ditches, or the repairs thereon, and in case of refusal or neglect to comply with said notice of the water-master having jurisdiction, said water-master is hereby empowered to have the necessary work done, and the cost of said work shall be assessed proportionately to the farming lands, lots, or parts of lots of said

Delinquents assessed.

delinquents benefited by said water, and the amount thereof shall be a lien upon said land, lots, or parts of lots as are city taxes.

SEC. 8. All persons so using water as to cause, through their failure or neglect, damage to any lot, street, sidewalk, ditch, bridge, or other property, shall be liable to a fine in any sum not exceeding fifty dollars for such offence, and to pay for all damages accruing thereby.

Fine.

SEC. 9. All persons are .hereby forbidden to run water or dig ditches across any of the public roads or streets within the limits of this corporation, for the purpose of conveying water for irrigation or other . purposes, unless they bridge, pave, or enclose the same under the direction of the Street Supervisor.

Ditches across public roads.

SEC. 10. The water-master having jurisdiction is • hereby required to notify all persons infringing upon this ordinance ; and, upon their refusing to comply with its requirements, he shall report them and their infringements to the Mayor or any alderman of this city, who shall cause the offenders to be brought before him, and, upon conviction, they shall be liable to a fine in any sum not exceeding twenty-five dollars for each offence, and to pay for all damages that may accrue therefrom.

Infringements.

SEC. 11. In cases where persons are obliged to convey water across grounds between their premises and a public water-ditch, which they are hereby authorized to do, they are hereby required to do so under the direction of the city water-master, and with the least possible injury to their neighbors' property, both in digging the requisite ditches and in managing

Ditches in private grounds.

the water therein; and for failure or neglect in so doing shall be liable to pay for all damages caused thereby. When public water-ditches pass through private grounds, the right of way therefor is hereby guaranteed; and any person having the right to use the water therefrom is hereby authorized to pass along said ditches, as occasion may require, during the time said person holds said right; said passing to be under the supervision of the water-master having jurisdiction.

SEC. 12. "An ordinance in relation to water-ditches and side-walks," passed March 3rd, 1860; and "An ordinance relating to the water and water-ditches Repealed. for the farming lands of Great Salt Lake City," passed March 5th, 1860, are hereby repealed.

———o———

CHAPTER XXXIV.

IN RELATION TO SETTING POSTS AND SECURING TEAMS.

SEC. 1. Be it ordained, by the City Council of Salt Lake City, that all persons owning buildings within the limits of said city are hereby required to set one or Where to more posts in the street, twenty-five feet from the front put posts. line of their lots. Where the water-ditches interfere, a variation may be made sufficient to clear such ditch; said posts must be set in a good substantial manner, suitable for securing horses or other animals.

SEC. 2.   If any person refuses or neglects to comply with the foregoing section of this ordinance, the corporation shall have the right to set said post at the expense of the owners of said building.

Refusal.

SEC. 3.   All persons are hereby forbidden to set sign, awning, or other posts on any of the side-walks of this city, except they set them sixteen feet from the street line of their lots ; and no sign or awning shall be less than eight feet above the grade of the side-walk ; *Provided:* That nothing in this section shall be so construed as to prohibit persons from setting posts on the side-walks opposite the corners of blocks, to prevent the trespassing of teams.

Awning, posts, etc.

SEC. 4.   Any person having charge of, or being the driver of, a team, shall, while such team is standing in the streets or any public place of said city, stand near the head of the same, or have hold of the lines attached to them, or otherwise secure them to some post or other substantial place of fastening prepared for that purpose.   Any person or persons violating this ordinance shall be liable to a fine in any sum not less than five nor more than fifty dollars for each offence.

Securing teams.

CHAPTER XXXV.

CONCERNING THE SIDE-WALKS ON NORTH TEMPLE STREET.

Be it resolved, by the City Council of Salt Lake City, that the side-walks on North Temple Street, in Salt Lake City, be and the same are hereby reduced in width to eight feet between the line of the lots and the water-ditches.

————o————

CHAPTER XXXVI.

SIDE-WALKS, SHADE TREES AND WATER-DITCHES IN PLOT D.

SEC. 1.   Be it ordained, by the City Council of Salt Lake City, that the side-walks in plot D of said city, shall be made ten feet wide, and that the inside edge of the water-ditches shall be the outside line of the side-walk, and all shade trees placed in the streets shall be set eight and a half feet from the line of the lots.

SEC. 2. Any person violating any portion of this ordinance shall be liable to a fine of not less than one, nor more than one hundred dollars for each offence.

———o———

CHAPTER XXXVII.

DIGGING IN THE STREETS.

———

SEC. 1. Be it ordained, by the City Council of Salt Lake City, that no person, without permission of said Council, shall take up, remove, or carry away, or cause to be taken up, removed, or carried away, any turf, stone, sand, clay, or earth from any street, public place, or highway in said city, under a penalty of not less than one, nor more than fifty, dollars for each offence.

Removing earth.

SEC. 2. Nothing in the preceding section shall be so construed as to prohibit any person from working the streets or digging water-ditches under the direction of the Street Supervisor.

CHAPTER XXXVIII.

DECLARING PUBLIC AND NAMING THE STREETS OF SALT LAKE CITY.

———

SEC. 1. Be it ordained, by the City Council of Salt Lake City, that all the streets as plotted in the several surveys of Salt Lake City shall be known by names as follows: The street running on the south side of what is known as the Temple Block of said city, shall be known by the name of South Temple Street, and the next one south as First South Street, and so on in regular order of number to the southern limits of said city. That the street running on the west side of said Temple Block be known by the name of West Temple Street, and the next one west as First West Street, and so on in regular order of number to the western limits of said city. That the street running on the north side of said Temple Block be known by the name of North Temple Street, and the next one north as First North Street, and so on in regular order of number to the northern limits of said city. That the street running on the east side of said Temple Block be known by the name of East Temple Street, and the next one east as First East Street, and so on in regular order of number to the eastern limits of said city.

South of Temple Block.

West of Temple Block.

North of Temple Block.

East of Temple Block.

L

SEC. 2. That the first street north of, and running parallel with, South Temple Street, east of First East Street be called Fruit Street ; that the second street north, running parallel, be called Garden Street; that the third street north, running parallel, be called Bluff Street; that the fourth street north, running parallel, be called Wall Street; that the fifth street north, running parallel, be called Prospect Street; that the sixth street north, running parallel, be called High Street; that the seventh street north, running parallel, be called Mountain Street; that the eighth street north, running parallel, be called Summit Street. That the first street east of Second East Street running north from South Temple Street be called Walnut Street; that the next street east, running parallel, be called Chestnut Street; that the next street east, running parallel, be called Pine Street; that the next street east, running parallel, be called Spruce Street ; that the next street east, running parallel, be called Fir Street; that the next street east, running parallel, be called Oak Street ; that the next street east, running parallel, be called Elm Street ; that the next street east, running parallel, be called Maple Street; that the next street east, running parallel, be called Locust Street; that the next street east, running parallel, be called Ash Street ; That the next street east, running parallel, be called Beech Street ; that the next street east, running parallel, be called Cherry Street ; that the next street east, running parallel, be called Cedar Street; that the next street east, running parallel, be called Birch Street; that the next street east, running parallel, be called Hickory Street; that the next street east, running parallel, be called Arch Street ; that the next street east, running parallel, be called Box Elder Street ; that the next street east,

North of South Temple and east of 2d East St.

Streets in Plot D and G.

running parallel, be called Cottonwood Street; that the next street east, running parallel, be called Quakingasp Street; that the next street east, running parallel, be called Poplar Street; that the next street east, running parallel, and being the extreme east street of Plot G. running north from South Temple Street, be called Willow Street. Streets in Plot E.

SEC. 3. That the street beginning at the north end of East Temple Street, running north to Arsenal Block, be called Arsenal Street; that the street commencing near the south end of Arsenal Street, running in a north-westerly direction, terminating on First West Street, be called Centre street; that the next street east running parallel with Centre Street, be called Beet Street; that the next street east, running parallel with Beet Street, joining the city wall, be called Back Street; that the street commencing at the eastern terminus of Third North Street, running directly north to Centre Street, be called Quince street.

That the street running on the east side of the Arsenal Block be called Strawberry Street; that the street running on the north line of said Arsenal block be called Currant Street; that the street running on the west line of said Arsenal block be called Pea Street; that the street running on the south line of said Arsenal block be called Grove Street.

That the street commencing at First North Street and the northern terminus of West Temple Street, running directly north, be called Carrot Street; that the street commencing at the northern terminus of Carrot Street, running west, be called Apple Street; that the street commencing at the western terminus of Apple Street, running north, intersecting Carrot Street, be called Melon Street; that the street commencing at the western terminus of Currant Street, running north to Quince Street, be called Citron Street.

That the street running from Arsenal Street, in a zig-zag course, to Grove Street, be called Crooked Street; that the street commencing at First North Street and terminating at the junction of Crooked and Strawberry Streets, be called Curve Street; that the street running from Centre to Currant Street be called Vine Street; that the street running from Centre to Vine Street be called Branch Street; that the street running from First North Street to Currant Street, nearly parallel with Vine Street, be called Grape Street; That the second street north of the Arsenal, running from First West to Back Street, be called Apricot Street; that the next street north, running from First West to Back Street, be called Plum Street; that the next street north, running from First West to Back Street, be called Peach Street; that the next street north, running from First West to Back Street, be called Pear Street; that the next street north, running from Centre to Back Street, be called Cane Street.

That the next street north, running from First West to Back Street, be called Short Street; and that the street running from Currant to Apricot Street be called Almond Street, and that the aforenamed streets be and are hereby declared public streets of Salt Lake City.

CHAPTER XXXIX.

RELATING TO BURNING WEEDS, RUBBISH, AND OTHER
COMBUSTIBLE MATERIALS.

Be it ordained, by the City Council of Salt Lake
City, that any person burning weeds, rubbish, or combustibles of any kind within the limits of said city,
except in the day time, between the hours of sunrise
and sunset, and the said burning be superintended by
some responsible person, and at a distance of not less
than forty feet from any building, fence, stack, or other
material liable to take fire, he shall be liable to a fine
in any sum not exceeding one hundred dollars, and
subject to pay all damages.

——o——

CHAPTER XL.

RIDING AND DRIVING OVER JORDAN BRIDGE.

Be it ordained, by the City Council of Salt Lake
City, that no person or persons shall be allowed to
ride or drive any animal faster than a walk across the
bridge over Jordan river, on North Temple Street ; nor
to drive upon said bridge more than thirty head of cattle, horses, or mules, at the same time ; nor more than
two loaded wagons at the same time ; nor to drive
cattle, horses, or mules upon said bridge for the pur-

pose of corralling or catching the same. Any person
not observing this ordinance shall be liable for each
offence to a fine of not less than one nor more than one
hundred dollars, and pay all damages. One half of
such fine shall go to the complainant and the other half
into the city Treasury.

———o———

CHAPTER XLI.

TRESPASS, AND CONCERNING ANIMALS RUNNING AT LARGE.

Trespass.

SEC. 1.　Be it ordained, by the City Council of Salt
Lake City, that any person who shall take down any
fence, or let down any bars, or open any gate so as to
expose any enclosure, or ride, drive or walk across the
premises of another, within the limits of said city, without permission of the owner or occupant thereof, shall
be liable to a fine in any sum not exceeding one hundred dollars for each offence.

Animals
at large.

SEC. 2.　No cattle, horses, mules, sheep, goats or
hogs shall be allowed to run at large within the limits
of this city, and all such animals so found may be
taken up by any person and driven to the pound, and
the owner of said animals shall be liable to pay a fine
in any sum not exceeding ten dollars for each animal.

Excep-
tions.

SEC. 3.　Nothing in the preceding section shall
be so construed as to prevent any of the citizens from
herding milch cows, work cattle, horses, mules, or other
animals on the unenclosed lands within said city.

CHAPTER XLII.

ESTABLISHING AN INSANE ASYLUM AND HOSPITAL.

Sec. 1. Be it ordained, by the City Council of Salt Lake City, that the buildings erected by the Corporation of Salt Lake City, situate on the south-east Location. quarter (¼) of section ten (10), Township one (1) south, range one (1) east of the first principal meridian, United States survey, Utah Territory, for the proposed Asylum and Hospital for said city, be accepted, and the same be established as a place for the use and treatment of the sick, also the treatment and safe-keeping of insane or idiotic persons.

Sec. 2. For the purpose of liquidating indebtedness on said buildings, and to complete the necessary improvements, and to carry into effect the provisions of the foregoing section, the sum of ten thousand dollars, Appropriation. or so much thereof as may be necessary, is hereby appropriated; and the City Auditor is hereby required to draw his warrant, or warrants, on the City Treasurer for the same, as directed by the Mayor.

Sec. 3. The management and conduct of the said Asylum and Hospital shall be under the control of a Superintendent appointed. superintendent, who shall be appointed by, and hold his office during the pleasure of the City Council.

Sec. 4. Said superintendent, within ten days after

Bonds.

being notified of his appointment, shall qualify by taking an oath to faithfully perform the duties of his office, and give bonds with security for the faithful performance thereof, in the sum of five thousand dollars, to be approved by the City Recorder and filed in his office.

Furnishing Asylum.

Keep a record.

SEC. 5. Said superintendent shall provide suitable furniture, beds and bedding, and such other things as may be necessary for said Asylum and Hospital; and shall employ a suitable person to act as steward, who shall keep an accurate account of all the expenditures incurred.   He shall also keep a book or record of the Asylum and Hospital, entering therein the name, time and place of birth, so far as can be ascertained, date of entrance, date of discharge or death of any inmate of said Asylum and Hospital, and perform such other duties as may be required by the superintendent or Hospital Physician; and make a full and complete report to the superintendent on the first day of each month.

Assistants.

Report.

SEC. 6.   The superintendent shall have authority to employ the services of such nurses or assistants as may be required from time to time, or as may be necessary for the proper care of inmates, and may discharge such employes at pleasure; and shall make a full and complete report to the City Council quarter-yearly, or oftener if required by said Council.

Physicians.

SEC. 7. There shall also be appointed by the Council one or more physicians for said Asylum and Hospital, who shall hold office during the will of, and shall receive such compensation as may be allowed by, said Council.

SEC. 8. All supplies furnished by said superintendent for the use and benefit of said Asylum and Hospital shall be placed in the care of a steward, who shall keep a strict account of, and be held responsible for, the same.

Steward.

SEC. 9. The Mayor shall visit said Asylum and Hospital, and it shall be his duty to enquire into the condition of the inmates, and make a thorough examination into the management of the Asylum and conduct of those employed, and give such instructions and make such changes and alterations as he may deem proper; and shall make a written report to the City Council once in every six months, or oftener if required by said Council, of the condition of the Asylum and Hospital, stating the amount expended for its conduct and management, together with such other information as he may deem proper.

Mayor to visit and examine.

Report.

SEC. 10. The physician shall provide and prescribe the mode and manner of treatment of the inmates of said Hospital and Insane Asylum, and keep a record of the diseases and direct the discharge of the inmates; and in case of the death of any inmate, make a record thereof, and notify, when practicable, the friends of the deceased. In the event of the death of any inmate of the Asylum or Hospital, the physician shall cause a suitable burial of the deceased and make a report of his doings to the City Council whenever required.

Duties of physician.

SEC. 11. The sick or adjudged insane shall be received into said Asylum or Hospital from any county in the Territory of Utah by satisfactory arrangements being made with the superintendent, by themselves, friends or the County Court of the county where such

Conditions of receiving sick.

M

afflicted persons reside, for the payment of the expense.

SEC. 12. All moneys or fees of every description, received from persons for care or treatment, as herein before provided, shall be paid into the City Treasury as received, without delay.

————0————

CHAPTER XLIII.

RELATING TO VEHICLES.

License.

SEC. 1. Be it ordained, by the City Council of Salt Lake City, that there shall be levied and collected a license upon all public vehicles using the streets of Salt Lake City, for trade or traffic, as hereinafter provided.

Manner of obtaining license.

SEC. 2. Applications for license under this ordinance shall be made in writing to the Mayor, and the amount hereinafter provided shall be paid in advance to the City Treasurer. All licenses shall be issued and signed by the Mayor and attested by the City Recorder, under the seal of the city. The Recorder shall keep an alphabetical list of licenses issued, stating the number, name, residence, amount paid, with such remarks as may be deemed necessary.

SEC. 3. On application being made, yearly licenses may be issued thereon as follows:

First. Upon a license to run an omnibus, $25.00.

Second. Upon a license to run a carriage, hack or other vehicle, drawn by two or more horses, $20.00.

Price of license.

. *Third.* Upon a buggy, cab, or other vehicle, drawn by one horse, $15.00.

Fourth. Upon a dray, truck, wagon, or other such vehicle, drawn by two or more horses, $12,00.

Fifth. Upon a dray, truck, wagon, or other such vehicle, drawn by one horse, $9.00.

SEC. 4. All public vehicles, licensed under this ordinance, shall be numbered with plain figures, painted on metalic plates, not less than three inches long and two inches wide, which shall always be kept conspicuously to view ; said numbers shall be furnished with the license by the City Recorder.

Numbered plates.

SEC. 5. The centre of Second South Street, between East and West Temple Streets, and between East Temple and First East Streets, is hereby set apart and established as a stand for all licensed carriages, hacks, cabs, or other such vehicles used for conveying passengers. The horses on both sides shall face East Temple Street, with their heads not less than ten feet back from the street crossings.

Stand for carriages.

SEC. 6. The east side of First East Street, between First and Second South Streets, and the east side of West Temple Street, opposite the market grounds, are hereby set apart and established as stands for licensed drays, trucks, wagons, and all other such vehicles.

Stand for drays, etc.

SEC. 7. It shall not be lawful for any licensed vehicle, when not actually employed, to be kept standing in any other part of the public highways of the City than those designated and set apart as stands for public vehicles, nor in front of any hotel, place of public business, or private residence without the express permission of the owners or occupants thereof.

SEC. 8. It shall not be lawful for any carriage, hack, cab, wagon, dray, truck, or other vehicle to be

Speed.

driven through any of the streets of Salt Lake City, at a greater speed than eight miles an hour, nor around the corners of any of the streets of said City at a gait that will endanger pedestrians. And all vehicles, when passing through or along any of the streets of said City shall, when meeting another vehicle, be driven to

Meeting other vehicles.

the right hand side of the way so as to pass clear of each other.

SEC. 9. Any person violating any of the provisions of this ordinance shall, on conviction thereof, be

Fine.

liable to a fine in any sum not exceeding fifty dollars for each offence.

SEC. 10. All ordinances or parts of ordinances

Repealed.

conflicting herewith are hereby repealed.

CHAPTER XLIV.

RELATING TO HOUSES OF ILL-FAME AND PROSTITUTION.

SEC. 1. Be it ordained, by the City Council of Salt Lake City, that any person or persons who shall be found guilty of keeping, or shall be an inmate of, any house of ill-fame or place for the practice of fornication, or adultery; or knowingly own or be interested as proprietor or landlord of any such house; or any person or persons harboring or keeping about his, her, or their, private premises, any whoremaster, strumpet or whore, knowing them to be guilty of following a lewd course of life, shall be liable to a fine Fine. for each offence not exceeding one hundred dollars, or imprisonment not exceeding six months, or both fine and imprisonment at the discretion of the court having jurisdiction. In a prosecution under this section, the person having charge of any house or place shall be deemed the keeper thereof.

SEC. 2. It shall be lawful, on the trial of any person before said court charged with either of the offences named in the preceding section, for the city to introduce, in support of such charge, testimony of the Testimony. general character and reputation of the person or place touching the offence or charge set forth in the complaint, and the defendant may likewise resort to testimony of a like nature for the purpose of disproving such charge.

SEC. 3. No person shall be incapacitated or excused from testifying touching any offence, committed by another, against any of the provisions set forth in the first section of this ordinance, by reason of his or her having participated in such crime; but the evidence which may be given by such person shall in no case be used against the person so testifying.

Evidence.

SEC. 4. The word adultery, as made use of in this ordinance, shall be construed to mean the unlaw. fully cohabiting together of two persons when either one or both of such persons are married; and the word fornication shall be construed to mean the cohabiting together of two unmarried persons.

Meaning of Adultery and Fornication.

———o———

CHAPTER XLV.

ESTABLISHING THE CITY SEAL

———

SEC. 1. Be it ordained, by the City Council of Salt Lake City, that the seal heretofore provided and used by and for Salt Lake City (1 & $\frac{15}{16}$ inches in diameter), the impression on which is a representation of a lamb in the centre, with the inscription—"Salt Lake City Seal, U. T.," (around the outer edge thereof) shall be and is hereby established and declared to have been, now is, and hereafter to be, the Seal of Salt Lake City.

Impression.

CHAPTER XLVI.

REGULATING THE MEASUREMENT OF MASON WORK,
PLASTERING, PAVING AND CUT STONE.

SEC. 1. Be it ordained, by the City Council of Salt Lake City, that all walls of mason work, whether of stone or adobies, shall be measured by solid or cubic Solid. measurement; also all flues, fire places, ovens, boilers, cooking ranges, grate settings, furnaces, copper settings, and other like works.

SEC. 2. That a perch of mason work shall be sixteen and a half cubic feet, including openings; Perch. and that six adobies, each twelve inches long, five inches and three quarters wide, and four inches thick, shall be, when laid in a wall, one foot.

SEC. 3. That all paving, flagging, plain plastering, hard finish, and rough casting, including openings, be measured by superficial measurement; also, all cut stone, planed, tooled, such as door steps, door sills, coping and hearth stone, those parts only which show when set; and that all window-sills, caps and water table be measured by running measurement.

CHAPTER XLVII.

IN RELATION TO DRUGS AND MEDICINES.

———

Labeling.

SEC. 1. Be it ordained, by the City Council of Salt Lake City, that all physicians, nurses, druggists, apothecaries or other persons, are hereby required to label the names of drugs and medicines in a plain and legible manner, in the English language; which they may put up or cause to be put up, before such drugs or medicines leave their possession.

Fine.

SEC. 2. Any person neglecting or refusing to comply with the foregoing section of this ordinance shall be liable to a fine in any sum not exceeding one hundred dollars, or imprisonment not exceeding six months, or both fine and imprisonment.

CHAPTER XLVIII.

RELATING TO GUNPOWDER, GUN COTTON AND NITRO-GLYCERINE.

SEC. 1. Be it ordained, by the City Council of Salt Lake City, that it shall not be lawful for any person or persons to keep, sell or give away, gunpowder, gun cotton, or nitro-glycerine, in any quantity without permission of the City Council ; *Provided*, any person may keep, for his own use, not exceeding five pounds of gunpowder, one pound of gun cotton, or one ounce of nitro-glycerine. *Permit.*

SEC. 2. All permits, when issued, shall be registered by the Recorder, and shall state the name and place of business, and date of permit, and the same shall not be granted for a longer time than one year; *Term of permit.* and no person to whom any permits may be issued, shall have or keep, at his place of business or elsewhere, within the city, (except in such places as may be approved by the City Council), a greater quantity of gunpowder or gun cotton than twenty-five pounds, *How to be sold.* and the same shall be kept in tin canisters or cases, and nitro-glycerine not to exceed five ounces, and in a situation remote from fires, lighted lamps or candles. Nor shall any person sell or weigh gunpowder, gun cotton, or nitro-glycerine, after the lighting of lamps or gas in the evening, unless in sealed canisters or cases.

It shall be the duty of every person to whom a permit shall be given to keep a sign at the front door of his place of business, with the word gunpowder painted or printed thereon in large letters.

Sec. 3. No person shall convey or carry any gunpowder exceeding one pound in quantity through any street or alley in the city, unless the said gunpowder is secured in tight cans, kegs or cases, sufficient to prevent the same from being spilled or scattered, and in no quantity exceeding one hundred pounds, except under the direction of a police officer.

Carrying through streets.

Sec. 4. A violation of any clause of this ordinance shall subject the offender to a fine, for each offence, in any sum not exceeding one hundred dollars.

Fine,

———o———

CHAPTER XLIX.

DECLARING THE TIME WHEN ORDINANCES AND RESOLUTIONS SHALL BE IN FORCE.

———

Sec. 1. Be it ordained, by the City Council of Salt Lake City, that all ordinances and resolutions, passed by said council, shall be in force from and after their publication, unless otherwise provided for.

Sec. 2. This ordinance to be in force from and after its publication.

CHAPTER L.

AUTHORIZING THE MAYOR TO SIGN PAPERS AND FOR
OTHER PURPOSES THEREIN MENTIONED.

———

Be it resolved, by the City Council of Salt Lake
City, that the Mayor is hereby authorized and empowered to sign his name officially, for and in behalf of said
City, and take the necessary oath or oaths, in entering, Taking oaths.
disposing of, or transfering land, or other business,
and to sign deeds, bonds, bills, notes, or obligations;
and, when the said Council authorize it, to borrow Borrow money.
money on the credit of said City; and to sign all other
agreements, documents, or papers authorized by said
Council, when the City is a party and his signature is
necessary to make the same valid; also hereby legaliz-
ing, sanctioning and ratifying such transactions of like Past transactions sanctioned.
and similar nature, which have heretofore been officially
signed by him.

CHAPTER LI.

VALIDATING THE REVISED ORDINANCES AND RESOLUTIONS.

SEC. 1. Be it ordained, by the City Council of Salt Lake City, that the foregoing fifty chapters are hereby declared the ordinances and resolutions of said City in force this 20th day of July A. D., 1875, revised and compiled, and shall be designated "The Revised Ordinances and Resolutions of Salt Lake City," and shall remain, and be in full force from and after the said 20th day of July, A. D. 1875.

Designation of Ordinances and Resolutions.

SEC. 2. All ordinances, and resolutions or parts thereof, ordained and passed prior to this 20th day of July, 1875, in conflict with the provisions of these revised ordinances and resolutions are hereby repealed. *Provided* always, that such repeal shall not affect or in anywise impair any right accruing or any liability, forfeiture, or penalty incurred under such repealed ordinances, or affect any suit, prosecution or proceeding begun or pending prior to the said repeal; but all rights forfeitures, liabilities, or penalties incurred under said ordinances, may be enforced the same as if such repeal had not been made; nor shall such repeal affect the right to any office or change the term or tenure thereof.

Repeal.

ERRATA.

www.ingramcontent.com/pod-product-compliance
Lightning Source LLC
Chambersburg PA
CBHW030832270326
41928CB00007B/1012